EDUCATION SERVICES SPECIALIST

BETH A. VIVALDI & SHIRLEY E. JOHNSON

Order this book online at www.trafford.com
or email orders@trafford.com

Most Trafford titles are also available at major online book retailers.

Print information available on the last page.

isbn: 978-1-4907-6602-7 (sc)
isbn: 978-1-4907-6604-1 (hc)
isbn: 978-1-4907-6603-4 (e)

Library of Congress Control Number: 2015918806

Trafford rev. 11/13/2015

 www.trafford.com

North America & international
toll-free: 1 888 232 4444 (USA & Canada)
fax: 812 355 4082

CONTENTS

INTRODUCTION TO
THIS HANDBOOK

Although each course within this handbook has numerous books published on the subject(s), the authors have scaled the information down to what has been determined "essential" information to complete the task of designing a course or curriculum. The original design was to address only those academic areas of knowledge needed to qualify for the GS-1700 series. The GS-1700 series is the government identified sequence for training and education occupations held within the administration. Although many military instructors may have the initial credentials and qualifications outlined in the job summary, many do not have the "24 hours of academics in the specialized areas in Curriculum Design, Instructional Design, Adult Learning, the Educational Psychology of Learners, and the Assessment/Evaluation of Academic Performance". This set of chapters was devised to "bridge" that knowledge gap. Therefore, it is envisioned, if you complete the courses [academically] as outlined in this handbook, which encompasses these five areas, you should be able to apply for eligibility in GS-1700 series positions.

Additionally, the book is also envisioned as a handbook to be used as a refresher and complement to those who are already in the field. There are instructors coming into our military academies who must take the mandated training on how to design courses and instruct before they are assigned to the academies or military organizations that are centered on instructing military subjects. For those, this handbook provides the reference material they need to teach others "how to teach".

However, further, in doing the research for jobs in this area, the authors found that there are many other civilian agencies (outside the government) that knowledge of these areas would certainly build upon the individual's resume and make them prospective candidates in the job market.

We decided to call it a handbook because the book provides only the foundational knowledge base in the specific areas that align with designing a course or curriculum. The information contained in this book is meant to be supplemented through the instructor by including up-to-date articles, Internet links, and relevant real-world experiences in the course syllabi. The authors believe this is the wave of the future: ONE book for an entire curriculum and supplemented by the instructor in the classroom or online.

CHAPTER 1

CURRICULUM DESIGN

Curriculum is used in a number of different ways by parents, educators, and businesses; however, without a complex curriculum, one that promotes thinking and reasoning will punish those students who have the greatest needs. Some see curriculum as the "academic stuff that is done to children in school" (Yates, 2000). Ronald C. Doll (1996), in his book, *Curriculum Improvement: Decision Making and Process*, goes further, stating: "The curriculum of a school is the formal and informal content and process by which learners gain knowledge and understanding, develop skills, and alter attitudes, appreciations, and values under the auspices of that school" (p. 15).

Curriculum is not just a list of content subjects taught over a period of time, on the contrary is an "academic plan" and a means to get students involved in their learning. According to Lattuca and Stark (2009), academic plans should include the purpose of the curriculum, content, sequence, instructional methods and resources, evaluation approaches, and how adjustments to the plan will be made based on experience or assessment data. According to Wilson (2005), curriculum

1

is defined as that which is taught in schools; a set of subjects, contents, and a program of studies. There are three types of curriculum: *taught, learned, and tested.* As shown in the next few paragraphs, we will compare and contrast these three types to a state's math curriculum for applicability.

Three Curriculum Types

Considering the Curriculum, n.d. defined taught curriculum as that which is presented in a formal instructional setting. The taught curriculum is a specific set of information presented by an instructor with the expectation that the student will learn the material. Learned curriculum is the set of material that is actually learned by the student. This curriculum determines what the student knows and understands about the world. This can be what was taught as well as material not formally presented. Tested curriculum is the material that instructors consider important enough to warrant assessment of material mastery. *Taught, learned, and tested curriculum* must be congruent in order to provide students with an effective educational experience. Dijkstra (2004) confessed, "the label *curriculum is* used to denote either the total of all courses given in a school or the content of the course program in a particular domain" (p. 149).

When designing a curriculum, an instructional designer will try to address the physical, cognitive, and affective development of the group of learners, taking into consideration the group's developmental age. You can look at curriculum design as the **macro-view** to designing a group of instruction to meet a need for a general audience; whereas instructional design normally refers to the *micro-view* of one specific course or design of instruction geared to a specific audience. To show how curriculum design and instructional design intersect, we will use the example of the curriculum combined in his handbook that aligns to the knowledge base for an Education Specialist (as defined by usajobs.gov).

> Example: The curriculum of the Education Specialist was designed to meet the needs of those individuals who either teach, or supervise those who teach, but have no formal training in any of the following areas:
>
> 1) Tests and measurement: Study of the selection, evaluation, administration, scoring, interpretation, and uses of group and individual aptitude, proficiency, interest, and other tests;
> 2) Adult education: Study of the adult as a learner, teaching-learning theories for adults, models and procedures for planning, designing, managing, and evaluating adult learning activities;
> 3) Educational program administration: Study of the foundation and methods in organizing for adult and continuing education programs;

4) Curriculum development or design: Study of the principles and techniques for development of curricula for adult or vocational education programs; and

5) Teaching methods: Study of teaching strategies and learning styles of the adult learner.

The category of learners for whom this handbook is envisioned includes:

- college professors;
- trainers/instructors in military/police/corrections academies;
- individuals who work in a training/educational capacity in the military, police, and corrections;
- individuals who train employees in corporations or supervise those who train in those type entities;
- individuals who work in an educational advising setting and train on specific subjects (resume writing, education or occupational selection, interviewing techniques, etc.;
- those who oversee the planning and implementation of training to a large organization of employees, i.e., military, police, corrections, corporations, etc.

> *GOAL: To provide instruction within a specific framework (certificate) that identifies this gap of information. Thus the specific courses devised within the curriculum meets the 24 hour additional course instruction that makes the individual eligible academically to apply for positions within the GS-1700 occupational series. Additionally, provides instruction to enhance the skills and close the educational gap of those who teach, supervise those who teach, or provide training oversight regarding the standards and criteria for institutions who specialize in one type of curriculum (e.g., military, police, corrections, corporations, etc.).*

An instructional design teaches you the dynamics needed to develop learning that is effective and stimulating. Once the courses have been selected for the curriculum (what to teach), then each course goes through an in-depth instructional design process that will identify not only what is essential to teach so your student will learn the subject BUT how to teach. "The way in which the curriculum is designed, especially how the content is structured, influences the instructional design" (Dijkstra, 2004, p. 153). In Chapter 2, the instructional design (ID) process is outlined in detail, and certainly this same process could be used for a curriculum plan. However, for this chapter, you will look at a process used for decades to devise curriculum, and is still being used today. The process is called a DACUM, an acronym for developing a curriculum and is "an internationally recognized job/occupational analysis technique that is widely used by industry practitioners, educators and consultants to effectively identify the duties, tasks, and related information required for job/occupation" (Norton, 2004, p. 3).

DACUM Process.

The DACUM process was devised by the Ohio State University Center on Education and Training for Employment. This process is much like a task analysis to dissect a particular occupation or specific job. If an individual has ever participated in a DACUM process, one will find there are variations in how this is accomplished, but most of the time, the same components exist. Using a facilitator, a panel of experts is convened who perform the particular job or occupation you are focusing on, and through their collaborative actions, develop a list of all the duties and tasks associated with the job. In other words, they evaluate their own job.

The difference between conducting a DACUM in an industry or business environment, and a DACUM for a curriculum or program within a college, is that the college must focus on identifying occupational programs that have enough employment opportunities within the workforce that will attract students. How does a college or university determine new program offerings? By reviewing environmental and market trends in their geographical area, and by conducting a **needs analysis,** the college/university can ascertain if the program is needed.

The next component in a DACUM process is to complete a Job/Occupational Analysis. The analysis to determine a new college program or curriculum focuses on an occupational AREA, which may also mean several related jobs. For example, if a college wants to offer a criminal justice program, they would first look at the many related jobs within that occupational field, i.e., police officers, corrections, private security, state administrative type jobs, and government enforcement jobs.

The duties and tasks are listed, and translated into a chart whereby the experts prioritize the tasks essential to accomplishing each job, and in the process, identify training topics. Normally, the same panel then VALIDATES these tasks by again, prioritizing how frequent the task is performed and how essential each task is to the actual job. You now have the framework for a developing curriculum and the corresponding instructional materials.

The DACUM is a cost-effective and efficient way of devising a curriculum to identify the major duties and related tasks included in an occupation, as well as, the necessary knowledge, skills, and traits. A **competency profile** is then devised whereby one would *cluster* related tasks. The process is followed by a "SCID (**S**ystematic **C**urriculum and **I**nstructional **D**evelopment) which is designed to quickly and systematically produce relevant, high-quality, competency-based instructional materials based on the job/occupational analysis developed using the DACUM process" (Norton, 1997, p. 46)

Upon reviewing one's setting, which might be a school, a college, a business, a commerce, or a government organization, determining what skills, knowledge, and individual behaviors will be taught is imperative. With the lack of an accurate determination of content, Norton (2004) claimed, two major critical and costly errors are likely to occur: "the "Curriculum What Errors," which include failing to teach what should be taught (the latest skills and techniques) and teaching what should not be taught (outdated skills and information) (p. 3).

So, why is a DACUM important to educational institutions? Our job is to continue to prepare our students for tomorrow's jobs, and enhance the skills required to operate in the 21st century, such as critical thinking, reasoning, logic, and problem-solving. In order to keep abreast with these changes, educators must keep curricula relevant to the current and future needs of business and industry.

CHAPTER 2

INSTRUCTIONAL DESIGN

The Origins of Instructional Design

The concept of instructional design evolved from the efforts in World War II, when the U.S. military was faced with the need to rapidly train large numbers of individuals to perform complex technical tasks in minimum time. Based on the research and theories of B. F. Skinner at the time, operant conditioning was at the forefront of "efficient and effective" training focusing on "observable behaviors". "The tasks were broken down into subtasks, and each subtask was treated as a separate learning goal" (Clark, 2010).

McNeil's (2006, p. 1) definition of instructional design is process oriented, "…The systematic process of translating general principles of learning and instruction into plans for instructional materials and learning" and "…The process by which instruction is improved through the analysis of learning needs and systematic development of instruction." On the contrary, Winters' (2002) definition is people oriented, "…The process by which information is systematically mapped, categorized, and organized to facilitate the transmission of information or skills to people" (p. 1). Additionally, McNeil (2006) provides definition of instructional design as a process, a discipline, and a science in the following manner:

- Instructional Design is the systematic development of instructional specifications using learning and instructional theory to ensure the quality of instruction. Instructional Design is the entire process of analysis of learning needs and goals and the development of a delivery system to meet those needs;
- Instructional Design is that branch of knowledge concerned with research and theory about instructional strategies and the process for developing and implementing those strategies; and
- Instructional Design is the science of creating detailed specifications for the development, implementation, evaluation, and maintenance of situations that facilitate the learning of both large and small units of subject matter at all levels of complexity. (para. 2)

After the war, the success of the wartime training model was replicated in business and industrial training, and to a lesser extent in the primary and secondary classroom. The approach referred to today as the "systems approach" is still common in the U.S. military. There are several different aspects that come into play when designing instruction. These are domains *of learning (Bloom's Taxonomy), learning theories, and instructional design theories.*

Bloom's Taxonomy

In 1956, a committee led by Benjamin Bloom published an influential taxonomy of what he termed the three domains of learning: Cognitive (what one knows or thinks), Psychomotor (what one does, physically), and Affective (what one feels, or what attitudes one has) (Bloom, Engelhart, Hill, Furst & Krathwohl, 1956). To date, these taxonomies still influence the design of instruction. In fact, the objectives for a course are designed using Bloom's Taxonomy.

During the latter half of the 20th century, learning theories began to be influenced by the growth of digital computers. In the 1970s, many instructional design theorists began to adopt an information-processing-based approach to the design of instruction. Later in the 1980s and throughout the 1990s cognitive load theory began to find empirical support for a variety of presentation techniques. In the 2000s computer based training and eLearning gave rise to Internet and online learning. Academicians purported, "learning must be more effective and efficient. This need has given rise to the instructional design process, a systematic planning method that results in successful learning and performance" (Morrison, Ross, & Kemp, 2004, p. 2).

Instructional Design (ID)

Instructional design should point out a qualitative management systems approach for continuous improvement while specifying the importance of both the learner's needs and processes required to accomplish the learning goal. Therefore, instructional design should be a quality management system directed towards meeting the needs of the learner and improving the efficiency of the learning process through the continuous evaluation and improvement of techniques, processes, and materials relative to instruction.

We determined within the design process, that shortfalls in content or subject matter can be identified and amplified for inclusion into the course design. "One of the essential factors that accounts for learning is instructional alignment. In other words, what the teacher intends to teach (objectives) matches the practice activities (various tasks and games), and is checked during assessment and closure" (Petersen & Cruz, 2004, p. 33).

Instructional design (ID) refers to the "systematic and reflective process of translating principles of learning and instruction into plans for instructional materials" (Smith & Ragan, 1999, p. 2). One way to look at how instructional design plays in the *learning process* is by understanding its components. *Instructional theories*, informed by *learning theory*, equal an *instructional design plan*. This plan can then be designed visually, called an *instructional design model*. ID models give structure and meaning to an instructional design problem and help the designer visualize how to approach designing the instruction to that context.

Learning theories (descriptive) are concerned with how one learns whereby instructional theories (prescriptive) focus on how one can ensure the desired learning occurs (Morrison et al., 2004). Learning theories are covered more in-depth in

Chapter 4 (Educational Psychology). The learning theories that are prominent in course design are:

(1) *Behaviorism.* Theorists of behaviorism see learning as an act of acquiring the correct response to stimulus that is extrinsically controlled by positive and negative reinforcement (Behaviorism, n.d.). This theory discounts the intrinsic motivation of the learner to learn or to build knowledge from experience and what that experience means to the learner.

(2) *Cognitivism.* The theorists of cognitivism see knowledge as constructed from interpretations of past experience. During this period, children are focused on the development of thinking and related intellectual abilities. Cognitive development occurs when the student attempts to make sense of his/her world. They actively select and process information about the world and construct a meaningful internal representation of their knowledge. Cognitivists believe learning occurs from discovery and the experience obtained is intrinsically controlled by the learner's motivation...teaching guides a learner through new experiences (Cognitive constructivism, n.d.).

(3) *Constructivism.* The constructivist learning approach examines the concept of learning as an active socially constructed environment. The constructivist facilitates learning by allowing the learner to integrate their previous knowledge, skills, and experience with new

ideas and skills so that the learner gains new knowledge and deeper understanding. To the constructivist, the function of the teacher is to develop the social skills of the learner and to structure collaborative learning opportunities with other learners (Social constructivism, n.d.). Learners construct their own meaning for different phenomena. The learner has the opportunity to conceptualize, organize, and focus on the topic building on skills to bridge the knowledge divide. Social constructivism is a mixture of the behaviorist and cognitivists theories with the addition of social interaction of peers.

The link between knowledge, teaching, and learning is vital; they cannot be totally separated. Each theory has weaknesses and strengths and focusing on only one theory limits the learning process because every student learns differently. The constant challenge for teachers is to bridge the gap between what they teach and what the students learn in the educational environment. Bridging the gap will increase knowledge and that bridge comes in the form of the instructional design.

Phases of the ID Process:

The primary phases of the ID process involves the "activities of analysis, strategy development, evaluation and revision" (Smith & Ragan, 1999, p. 11). Reiser (2001) stated:

Over the past four decades, a variety of sets of systematic instructional design procedures (models) have been developed.....Although the specific combination of procedures often varies from one instructional design model to the next, most of the models include design, development, implementation, and evaluation of instructional procedures and materials intended to solve those problems. (p. 58)

However, current ID scholars (Merrill, 2002; Sims & Jones, 2002; Tennyson & Spector, 1998) suggested the ID process reflected in many ID models be iterative rather than linear, allowing the designer to enter the process at any point depending on the learning situation. In addition, it is agreed by these scholars that most learning problems do not require that each and every step depicted by the instructional design models need to be followed in order to produce an effective course design. However, all instructional designers who are novice to this discipline start to learn about the process using the ADDIE model. The components of effective lesson plans per the ADDIE instructional design model include pre-instructional activities, presentation of the material, listings of necessary materials, assessment, reinforcement and follow-up. The ADDIE acronym stands for Analysis, Design, Development, Implementation and Evaluation. The analysis stage is used to determine the learner's needs and objectives. The design stage lists the materials used to reach the objective. The development stage creates the materials needed to reach the objective. The implementation stage is used to present the materials to the student. The evaluation stage is used to assess how well the materials helped the students accomplish the objective. Evaluation is used at each stage of the model as feedback for continuous improvement.

In this chapter, the ID model, or process, will be explained in detail. There are several iterations of the design process by ID scholars. For example, Smith and Ragan (1999) defined the ID process in 3 stages rather than the 5 outlined by the ADDIE process. They promote Analysis, Strategy and Evaluation as the 3 main stages.

The Analysis stage also incorporates the analysis of the learner, the context, and the task analysis. Morrison, Ross, and Kemp (2004) defined the ID process in a circular design with several components. According to the authors, before any instructional design begins, one must identify the problem. The ID process is used when it is envisioned that a performance problem can be solved by training or instruction (Morrison et al., 2004; Smith & Ragan, 1999). So the question arises, how does one determine if the problem identified requires additional training, or it is a problem that training *CAN NOT* fix? Example:

A Call Center is the life blood of many companies. This is the first time a client has interaction with the company therefore, the customer service they experience is critical to gaining new business. In this example, the clients have expressed their dissatisfaction of the wait time to get a call center person to answer. The lines are almost always busy OR the client waits a long time before somebody answers. Is this a training problem? The problem is that the call center people are not answering the phones in a timely manner. Is it because they are chatting about personal business, or is it that they are taking too long with each customer, or is it a lackadaisical attitude towards picking up the phone in a timely fashion? These are areas that could warrant additional training in customer service techniques, which would require designing the training using the ID process. But taking the example farther, what if there are only 2 lines coming into the call center. Then no amount of training can fix the problem. The call center needs more lines, and possibly more operators to handle the volume of calls in a timely fashion.

Before the authors jump into the ADDIE process, they need to define the terms of training versus instruction. Many people use these interchangeably, but scholars (Driscoll, 2005; Reigeluth, 1999; Smith & Ragan, 1999), within the ID field will stress that the terms are very different. Training "refers to those instructional experiences that are focused upon individuals acquiring very specific skills that they will normally apply almost immediately" (Smith & Ragan, 1999, p. 2). Instruction is "the deliberate arrangement of learning conditions to promote the attainment of some intended goal" (Driscoll, 2005, p.332). For the purpose of this book, we are concerned with learning the process of designing "instruction", which is why we have included an entire chapter in this handbook (Chapter 4) on learning theories and learning styles.

ADDIE

When designing instruction, professional instructional designers (Smith & Ragan, 1999) stated the following assumptions that underlie the process:

1. To design instruction, the designer must have a clear idea of what the learner should learn as a result of the instruction;
2. There are principles of instruction that apply across all age groups and all content areas. For example, students must participate actively, interacting mentally as well as physically, with material to be learned;
3. Evaluation should include the evaluation of the instruction as well as the evaluation of the learner's performance. Information from the evaluation of the instruction should be used to revise the instruction in order to make it more efficient, effective, and appealing;

4. When the purpose of assessment is to determine whether or not learners have achieved learning goals, the learners should be evaluated in terms of how nearly they achieve those instructional goals rather than how they "stack up" against their fellow students; and

5. There should be congruence among goals, learning activities, and assessment. Along with the learner's characteristics and learning context, learning goals should be the driving force behind decisions about activities and assessment. (p. 18)

Analysis Phase

According to McGriff (2001), the analysis phase is used to identify the learner's problems and determine the learner's objectives. "Instructional designers must become clever investigators, examining the characteristics of the potential users, the learning environments, the perceived need for the instruction, and the instructional task before investing time and resources in the costly production of instructional materials" (Smith & Ragan, 1999, p. 31).

Needs assessment.

In order to determine whether or not there is a need for instruction, you must conduct a needs assessment. At the conclusion of a needs assessment, the reasons for developing the instruction should become very clear. Morrison, Ross and Kemp (2004) propose a very lengthy 4 phase process: Phase

1 is the planning process whereby one would determine who will participate in the study, i.e., the target audience and the approach to collecting the data. Phase 2 (Collecting the Data) involves whether or not you will interview your participants, send out questionnaires, or have a focus group. Phase 3 (Analyzing the Data), after the data is collected, requires one to use a system that prioritizes the needs identified in Phase 2. This will help identify and set goals for the instruction. Phase 4 compiles the report, which the end product will identify the problem(s). Therefore, if the problem(s) identified can be **FIXED** by instruction, then the instructional designer moves forward with the ADDIE process.

Smith and Ragan (1999) take a simpler, more consolidated approach to conducting a needs assessment. In fact, they describe 3 types of needs assessment conditions that calls for 3 different types of models: (1) Discrepancy-Based Needs Assessment Model is one that presumes the learning goals are identified and there is already instruction in place that relates to these goals (p. 32). However, the assessment is done to evaluate what is in place and to determine what must be modified; (2) the Problem-Solving, Problem-Finding Model (p. 35) that supposes there is a definite problem that needs to be addressed; and (3) the Innovation Model (p. 36) that requires a refocus on the goals and the instruction to include new goals to align with either new laws or new mandates on how to do business. Once the Needs Assessment is completed and you have identified the problem(s) you move into the instructional analysis of the learner and the context in which your instruction will be delivered.

Learner and contextual analysis.

Learners have a multitude of different traits or characteristics. Therefore, it is critical for the designer to identify those characteristics that are crucial to achieving the desired objective(s). "Heinrich, Molenda, Russell and Smaldino (1999) suggested that designers initially consider 3 categories of learner characteristics: general, specific entry, and learner styles" (Morrison et al., 1999, p. 37). General characteristics are variables such as gender, age, work experience, education and ethnicity. "Specific entry characteristics are prerequisite skills and attitudes that learners must possess to benefit from the training" (Morrison et al., 1999, p. 58). The level of instruction (entry level versus advanced level) is dependent on the learner's skills, aptitudes and attitudes, as well as their life experience(s). Lastly, learning styles play an important part in making the designed instruction engaging and interactive for the learner. There have been a multitude of studies (Spiro, Feltovich, Jacobson, & Coulson, 1995; Feltovich, Spiro, Coulson, & Feltovic, 1996) on how recognizing different learning styles and incorporating the various methodologies in the design of instruction, leads to increased retention and learning of the concepts or tasks being conveyed. According to Driscoll (2005), instruction should include activities for all types of learners using varying methods and modes using the same information, thus the repetition allows for better retention.

Personal and social characteristics of the learner should also be considered when designing instruction. Not only the age of the learner but the maturity level should be noted. Motivation and attitude towards the subject is essential for retaining the information; special talents such as the learner's mechanical abilities, previous work experience, health aspects, disabilities, and physical fitness should all be taken into consideration.

One last consideration when analyzing your learners is to recognize those groups who are classed as culturally diverse; to include minorities, learners with disabilities, and adult learners. Culturally diverse learners may not understand the English terminology in the same way as native born Americans, and they may have English as a second language (ESL), thus their interpretation of certain words may be different than the masses. Learners with disabilities need to be identified so that the design of the instruction includes activities that include modifications specifically for them. When conducting the analysis, you may want to bring in a specialist that can work with this group and thus make them part of the instructional planning team.

There have been a lot of studies completed on adult learners, their motivations and the strategies for teaching and learning to this particular group. Andragogy is known as the set of principles that define adult learners. This area will be covered in depth in Chapter 3. Look at the below scenario, which will assist one in the completion of a Learner Analysis.

Most learner analysis will be quite extensive (approximately 5 pages) to adequately address all the characteristics of the learner. Using the scenario that we want to devise a course on ethics for a police academy, we would look at the following:

1. The general characteristics of the targeted learner: This would include the age range, the ethnic diversity, the range of longevity for the officers within the department who will receive the instruction, adaptive technology for any handicapped individuals, and any translation devices required;

2. The specific entry competencies, academic or training information, or personal and social characteristics of the learners: This would include addressing their skills in computer literacy, their academic levels, their personal characteristics to include motivation and learning factors, and their professional and personal goals to achieve success with the course, and their learning styles and preferences;

3. The orienting context related to the identified learning need: This area addresses the knowledge, skills, and attitudes the learner brings to the instruction because it is important to know exactly what the learner expects to take away from this instruction;

4. Resource factors to be allocated to the project: This area addresses where the course will be conducted and its design as far as totally in the classroom or portion(s) of it on the web. When will be the start date, how long will it take, when will it end, and will they need skills to access the course if it is on the internet at any time; and

5. The transfer/application context related to the identified learning need: This area addresses the goal of the instruction and the strategies that will be employed to enhance retention of the information.

Contextual analysis.

According to Smith and Ragan (1999), "An in-depth investigation into what the environment is like where instruction will be implemented helps to ensure that the instruction will, indeed, be used in that environment" (p. 37). The contextual analysis phase looks at where this training takes place (i.e., room, warehouse, outside environment, etc.), and aspects associated with the area the instruction will take place. Some examples would include: lighting, room size, noise, temperature, seating capacity, alignment of the seating for each student, equipment to be used in the instruction, hours it will be offered, and how long each instruction module will take. Certainly, the above list is not all inclusive and as you analyze the particular environment, you may possibly discover many other aspects that might affect the design of your instruction.

Along with identifying the actual environment where the instruction will take place, an instructional designer must acknowledge there are "learning conditions" that correlate with good learning practices. Gagné (1985) specifies these conditions as:

1. Gaining the attention of the student with various methods of presenting the new information;

2. Informing the learner of the objective so there is an understanding of why they are learning this new information;

3. Stimulating the recall of prior learning through various instructional techniques so they can see why the new information has relevance;

4. Presenting the stimulus because every type of learning requires some type of stimulus. "The stimulus presented as an instructional event depends on specifically what is to be learned" (p. 252);

5. Providing learning guidance which supports the semantic encoding internal process making the stimulus meaningful and relevant;

6. Eliciting performance whereby the learner now is required to demonstrate in some fashion, the newly learned capability;

7. Providing feedback to the learner to ensure they understand the correct way to perform the new capability; and

8. Assessing the learner's performance to ensure that the instruction has been learned and retained.

In order to ascertain that you have identified all or most of the learning environment aspects that may affect the design of your instruction, you should either observe, survey, or interview your potential learners to get the most accurate data possible.

Contextual Analysis using the scenario already identified: Ethics course for a Police Academy. These would be some of the considerations to be viewed in detail in your analysis.

Lighting
Noise
Temperature
Seating
Accommodations
Equipment
Transportation

The last segment in the analysis phase involves the tasks involved to learn the content of the unit or course. This is the most critical step in the design process because success of the course or unit depends on the "concise definition of the content that is the object of the instructional materials" (Morrison et al, 2004, p. 78)

Task analysis.

Upon completing a needs assessment, one normally compiles a list of learning goals. Learning goals are statements that the learner should be able to do at the end of the instruction. These goals should reflect clearly the capabilities the learners will possess, or be able to do upon the completion of the instruction. Although there are educators who tell you that they do not use learning goals, more than likely they have not been formally written down, but they are there. For example, one of the goals of this course is for you to conduct a task analysis. That is a pretty vague goal. But in our mind, we know that (1) we want the learner to have an understanding of the process of task analysis (2) to be able demonstrate how to complete a task analysis from an intended specific goal to specific learning outcomes that meet that goal, and be able to apply that process to a relevant problem in a real-world work environment. Now you know exactly what we want but if we did not express that to you in those terms, you would be trying to read our mind as to "what specifics are we talking about and how do I go about doing it?" That is why the next step in the process, after identifying the goal, is to identify the learning outcome that the goal represents.

Example: The goal is to conduct a task analysis. ONE of the associated learning outcomes is to recall the steps of the process for a task analysis. The term "recall" normally means reciting back and the mental process is normally memorization. So after rehearsal and repetition, you can normally recall the process pretty easily.

But what if the goal is to comprehend the criticality of the task analysis in the realm of instructional design? Comprehend means that you not only recall all of the components of the process but WHY each component is important to the overall design of the instruction. You would also use Bloom's taxonomy (which we will discuss) to explain the different learning levels of learning in the cognitive domain. In other words, the term that we use to describe a learning outcome also lends to the level of difficulty to learn that objective.

Bloom's taxonomy (Bloom, Engelhart, Furst, Hill, & Krathwohl, 1956) is the seminal work on how to devise learning objectives in the three domains that he named: cognitive domain (dealing with understanding), affective domain (dealing with emotions and affections), psychomotor (dealing with hands-on). Bloom's versions have been modified by scholars over time but the basic concepts of learning have not changed. One of the most noted scholars in instructional design is Robert Gagne (1985) who divided the possible learning outcomes into five domains which includes: verbal information (declarative knowledge), intellectual skills, cognitive strategies, attitudes, and psychomotor skills (Smith & Ragan, 1999, p. 65). As he outlines that each learning task requires a different mental process, it also requires a specific learning condition. In other words the learning task MUST be supported with the "condition" that supports that learning.

To conduct a task analysis, we will use the information-processing analysis as defined by Smith and Ragan (1999). By analyzing the goal in this fashion, you can break it down into its components to ensure that the student learns what is needed to attain the goal.

Example: The goal is to learn how to make a pizza, using the information-processing analysis procedure.

1. Read and gather as much information as possible about the task and content implied by the goal. In making a pizza, you would want to know certain terminology that is indicative of making a pizza. For example, "kneading the dough" is terminology for this particular task that is specific to how to make the dough;

2. Convert the goal into a representative "test" question. For example, in the learning goal identified, you could ask "what are the ingredients that must be used to make a pizza?" or;

3. Give the problem to several individuals who know how to complete the task and do one or several of the following activities:

   a. Observe them completing the task and ask them to talk aloud as they complete each step of the task.

   b. As you observe them completing the task, write down all the steps, or videotape the steps.

   c. Have the individual complete the task and then ask them to write down the steps for you;

4. Review the written steps or replay the videotape of the expert completing the task and ask questions about the process;

5. If more than one expert is used in steps 1-4, identify the common steps and decision points used by the experts in steps 3-4. Even experts complete the same task a little differently. Also, they complete the task without knowingly thinking about each independent step which is why you want to find the common steps between 2 such experts to determine how you will approach the task;

6. Identify the shortest, least complex path for completing the task, noting factors that require this simpler path. Do NOT include irrelevant information that does not specifically address how to do the task;

7. Note factors that may require a more complex path or more steps (these may indicate decision points). For example, making the sauce for the pizza can be a complex task in itself requiring a separate decision point, i.e., make the sauce and then spread it onto the pizza dough or make the sauce and put it over the other ingredients, thus it is last on the pizza;

8. Select the circumstances, and the simpler or more complex paths, that best match the intention of your goal;

9. List the steps and decision points appropriate to your goal; and

10. Confirm the analysis with other experts. (pp. 69-71)

Now that you have dissected the goal into the various tasks, the next step is to do the same thing with each TASK. For example, the first TASK in making a pizza is to determine what ingredients are needed for not only the dough but the pizza sauce. Some of the factors that also must be considered before you begin is what size is the pizza, how thick will be the crust, and what toppings are you going to use? These are all prerequisites to accomplishing the tasks, and thus accomplishing the goal.

Writing the Learning Objectives.

The learning objective can also be called an instructional objective. The objective tells the designer exactly what the learner should be able to do once the instruction is completed. A well designed objective will state who your audience is *(A)*, *the behavior (B) that the learner will demonstrate AFTER the instruction, the conditions (C) under which the performance is to be assessed, and the degree (D) of accuracy or proficiency the learner* must display upon completion of the instruction. Again we look to Bloom's Taxonomy so the verbs used in stating the behavior in the objective, conform to the level of learning: knowledge, comprehension, application, analysis, synthesis, and evaluation.

Morrison et al. (2004) claimed, "Objectives are normally grouped into 3 major categories (or domains): cognitive, psychomotor, and affective" (p. 108). The cognitive domain includes objectives that relate mainly to information or knowledge to be learned, mental aspects of solving, predicting, and other intellectual aspects of learning. The psychomotor domain deals with skills requiring the use of physical activities whereby the learner must perform, manipulate, or construct something. Lastly, the affective domain concerns attitudes, values, and emotions. Each one of the domains must be assessed to determine if the student actually LEARNED what the goal and objective outlined. The affective domain is the hardest objective to measure. Most instructional objectives that are written in the ID process concentrate on the cognitive domain.

Examples of objectives written in the ABCD format.

COGNITIVE DOMAIN:

Knowledge Level: *Using the prescribed cookbook (C) the student (A)* will *define* the *list of ingredients required (B) to* make an *(D) eatable 10 inch pizza with toppings of cheese and pepperoni.*

Comprehension Level: *From memory* (C), the *student (A)* will *describe (B)* the process to make a 10 inch pizza with toppings of cheese and pepperoni in 5 *minutes (D).*

Application Level: *From memory* (C), the *student (A)* will *demonstrate (B)* making a 10 inch pizza with toppings of cheese and pepperoni in 5 *minutes (D).*

Analysis Level: The *student (A)* will *compare and contrast (B)* two different methods of making a pizza *using (1) the ingredients from one recipe versus a recipe using whole wheat ingredients for the crust (C)*. *With 100% accuracy (D)*, the student will be able to differentiate between the two pizzas based on the use of the different ingredients for the pie crust,

Synthesis Level: *Using the knowledge of the basic foundations that the student learned to make a pizza (C), the student (A)* will *create (B)* a new pizza by *selecting 5 new ingredients to add to the formula (D)*.

Evaluation Level: *From memory and based on past experience (C)* the *student (A)* will make *2 pizzas using the same ingredients* (C). The student will taste both pizzas and *assess which one is better than the other and defend with exacts (D)*. *Why one was chosen over the other (B)*.

PSYCHOMOTOR DOMAIN:

Given the list of ingredients and a recipe for making a pizza (C), the student (A) *will mix the dough ingredients, roll out the pie crust, mix the ingredients for the sauce, spread the sauce over the pie crust, put the cheese and pepperoni on the top of the pizza sauce (B)*, and *bake the pizza in the oven for 20 minutes, checking it frequently so it does not burn (D)*.

AFFECTIVE DOMAIN:

Given a list of ingredients and a recipe for making a pizza (C), the student (A) *engages in making a pizza with enthusiasm, and agrees (B)* that the final product *tastes like a pizza (D).*

Summary

The authors have covered the first phase of instructional design which included identifying the problem and keying in on the goal needed to possibly resolve the problem. By analyzing the audience and the context in which you will deliver the instruction, you have narrowed the content needed that will specifically address the problem. You must remember that during this analysis, you will also discover the level of knowledge the learner will already possess, if any, which dramatically effects where your start of instruction will begin. For example, you would not address in the content of instruction to "make a pizza" if the individual is already versed in making pasta sauce. If they already know that part of the content, then you would gloss over the "how to make the sauce" portion of your instruction. When we cover adult learning in Chapter 3, this is important to understand because many adult learners will bring "life experience" to the course, which equates in some fashion to prior learning in a particular subject.

Once the learner and context has been analyzed, and you have identified the content that must be covered to address the problem, then you complete the task analysis of exactly what is going to be taught. The writing of the objectives in the ABCD format (see Appendix C) aligns with the content and what is expected to be learned by the student at the completion of the instruction, and to what proficiency, in order to address the problem already identified that suggested the need for this instruction.

You are now ready for the design and development phase of the instruction.

Design and Development of Instruction

According to McGriff (2001), the design phase is used to plan a strategy for developing course instructions to determine how to reach the objective; the development stage produces lesson plans and course materials needed to develop the instructions;

Sequencing the Instruction.

As we discussed the progressive learning we designed into the objectives using Bloom's taxonomy, an instructional designer must look at how to sequence the instruction that will relate to each of these objectives. "Sequencing is the efficient ordering of content in such a way as to help the learner achieve the objectives" (Morrison et al, 2004, p. 137). There are several different ways to sequence instruction based on what you are teaching, but for this course we will focus on only two that are the most popular. The first method was devised by Robert

Gagne (1985) which is based on the "building block premise", learning basic skills and the subsequent skills that link to the latter ones just learned, thus the building block. The second approach to sequencing was devised by Charles Reigeluth, known as the Elaboration Theory, but both authors can be said to be proponents of the systems instructional approach. The system instructional approach has been a popular way to sequence the learning of instruction for many decades and still today, there are numerous research studies showing empirical evidence that the systems approach to instruction promotes learning and retention (Borthwick, Jones, & Wakai, 2003; Duncan, 1996; Eklund & Woo, 1998; Hashim, 1999; Kidney & Puckett, 2003; Merrill, 2002, 2007; Reyes, 1990; Sims & Jones, 2003; Tonn, Hemrick, & Conrad, 2006; Wallen, Plass, & Brunken, 2005).

Using a part-whole-part technique, which is breaking the task down into subtasks (Clark, 1999), allows the learner to make meaning and connections of the information learned. This is the basis of the systems instructional approach of Gagné and Reigeluth. Their theories proposed introducing content to the learner in a sequenced format via digestible chunks of information to avoid a cognitive overload. The first introduction of the topic is from a very general viewpoint which serves as an *advance organizer*. New information is presented in context so the learner can easily recall the information from the schema.

Both theorists believe in introducing information to be learned from a broad, general concept followed by more detailed, specific concepts. Gagné's (1985) theory focuses on tasks and skills to be learned that will eventually combine to produce the entire concept at the end of the learning session. Gagné's learning hierarchy "refers to a set of component skills that must be learned before the complex skill of which they are a part can be learned" (Driscoll, 2005, p. 358). Subjects or segments dealing with "How to" fall within the instructional purview of Gagné's theory.

Reigeluth's elaboration theory (1999) is designed for use in learning concepts that have many related complex tasks or principles (p. 426). In other words, the "sequence instruction" is a holistic approach to the task, whereby "each version of the task is a class or group of complete, real world performances of the task" (p. 443). One can see Piaget's (1971) influence on Gagné's work through the concept whereby "knowledge of certain subjects can only be gained when all the components of that knowledge are present and properly developed" (Vander Zanden, 2003, p. 153).

Although the sequencing approach of the two theories differs significantly in the flexibility of how the content is learned, the basic concept is identical. For example, Gagné (1985) proposed that each concept must be learned through the progressive achievement of each task, connecting each segment of learning to the next segment.

In contrast, Reigeluth's (1999) blueprint for learning is more flexible. His approach to learning the topic can be either in a top-down configuration (spiral sequencing) or weaving across several concepts (topical sequencing), thus allowing the learner to make connections between several bigger concepts simultaneously. He further defined the learning of heuristic tasks (principles, guidelines, and causal models) versus procedural tasks (as defined by path analysis). Within Reigeluth's approach, these concept areas can also be sequenced and elaborated either individually, depending on the content to be learned, or simultaneously, which is called "multi-strand sequencing." For example, when instructing police on traffic stop procedures or responding to an incident such as a domestic dispute, the Reigeluth theory would seem more appropriate to this type of instruction whereby the concept and principles are stressed first, followed by the task or path analysis. Although both approaches seem to differ, the authors leave the door open to allow for the inclusion of constructive type activities and learning approaches, which will be addressed later in this book.

Both theorists advocate stipulating clear and concise goals and objectives since this strategy has been proven to improve learning outcomes (Clark, 1999). Acceptance of defining learning objectives is now coming into question, especially by those who adhere to the constructivist approach to learning. They condone stating very specific instructional objectives in learning materials because it destroys the holistic nature of the goal by decontextualizing the skills (Driscoll, 2005). Spector, Ohrazda, Van Schaack, and Wiley (2005) note that research from the 1970s revealed that objectives, as well as sequencing, did not have the impact in the learning process as previously believed (p. 221). However, Clark and Driscoll are in agreement with Gagné and Reigeluth, and contend instructional objectives are effective in drawing the learner's attention and energy to the intended outcome.

Gagné (1985) and Reigeluth (1999) also advocate categorizing learning goals according to learning outcomes, thus providing meaning and relevance to the content to be learned. Starko (2005) reiterates this premise stating that "learning in pursuit of a goal makes the learning purposeful. Tying information to prior knowledge, understanding, and affect, makes it meaningful" (p. 15).

Instructional Strategies: The Systems Approach to Learning.

In the systems approach, conditions of learning are specified to optimize knowledge acquisition. The learning or instructional strategies employed are a combination of practices that have been previously proven to enhance learning. For example, the theory of meaningful, reception learning advocates the use of advance organizers to serve as a bridge between what the learner already knows and what the learner needs to know. Additionally, the systems approach subscribes to the construct of assimilation, where an idea or concept is absorbed into the mind and combined with schema that contains similar ideas and concepts, thus forming a new and expanded understanding of the idea. This concept directly supports Vygotsky's (1978) zone of proximal development (ZPD), which describes the area of learning growth between what the learner already knows, and the unknown information to be learned. Therefore, social interaction is not only used as a strategy for learning but also becomes integral for use in scaffolding and reciprocal learning.

Bandura's (1977) cognitive learning theory is also posited in the information-processing theory which advocates strategies such as modeling, social interaction, and real-world experiences in order to make appropriate connections between existing knowledge and new knowledge. These strategies have survived the test of time and are confirmed by Gagné (1985) and Reigeluth (1999) when prescribing learning conditions that must be present to enhance retention and support deep learning. Teaching strategies such as modeling, task oriented examples, demonstrations, paraphrasing, outlines, mnemonics, retrieval cues, and encoding procedures provide the learner with various opportunities to frequently practice the task or concept, and receive continual feedback.

In the systems approach to instruction, the teacher maintains control and structures the activities to guide the student to "master the content". This approach allows the teacher to eventually fade out scaffolding techniques. As has been evidenced by examining the systems approach to instruction through the lens of Gagné (1985) and Reigeluth (1999), effective learning can be achieved through sequenced learning instruction (Li & Liu, 2005). Those who advocate the systems approach attempt to select activities and topics that are relevant and motivating to the student. The motivation for the student lies in the consistent feedback by the instructor and the feeling of empowerment by accomplishing the activity.

Developing the Instruction

Instructional Strategies as defined via Learning Theories

An instructional designer cannot develop effective and efficient instruction without having knowledge of how people learn. By identifying the learning theory(s), one can correlate the correct instructional strategies to be employed for teaching the content in the most effective and efficient manner. Since there are numerous learning theories in the academic arsenal that have been shown to enhance teaching and learning, this area of study will be covered in depth in Chapter 4, Educational Psychology. For this section, we will briefly cover some of the most prominent learning strategies as they correlate with various prominent learning theories.

Under the theory of Behaviorism, there are certain design strategies that support the concept of behavior modification through reinforcements. The learning activities and strategies focus on behavioral patterns that are continually repeated until it becomes automatic, with no mental thought when doing the procedure. Reinforcements are used to strengthen or weaken the behavior. Aspects of behaviorism can be found to provide the foundation for many subjects taught at the elementary and secondary levels of education, and then expanded on through cognition principles presented at the post-secondary level.

The three principles for teaching new behaviors that have met with success are: *shaping, chaining, and fading* (Driscoll, 2005). *Shaping,* which involves positive reinforcement presented each time the desired behavior is exhibited and with immediacy, has shown to be extremely effective. Shaping also involves cues attached to behaviors, and with the gradual strengthening of the learned relationship between the cue and the behavior, the link becomes very strong.

The next principle, *chaining,* is a building block process, taking each new behavior and building upon each. For example, when a student completes the first objective in a learning segment and shows performance without fault, then the next assignment should expand a little in its difficulty level. Adding a simulation or game to the next assignment or a different technique to expand on the one just learned supports the principle of chaining.

The last principle, *fading,* is based upon cues attached to the learned behavior so the learner can distinguish when the behavior is to be performed, and the "fading" of the cues will not negate the learned behavior. The "fading" is normally experienced through a passage of time. Therefore, when something is learned such as making a pizza, and the individual continues to practice the techniques and procedures learned, there is no constant praise, money, or promotions to make the individual continue to do the procedures correctly. However, by doing it correctly, this is "fading."

Under the theory of Cognitivism which is concerned with learning processes, there are several different approaches to take. One of the more known and practiced approaches to advance cognition is the systems approach of instruction, as previously discussed earlier in the sequencing approach to designing instruction. In the cognitive theorist's view, the acquisition of information impacts cognitive structures, thus the processing and storage information becomes a building-block process. Driscoll (2005) uses the analogy of the computer to describe the information processing sequence.

However, in order to appreciate the systems approach to instruction, you must fully understand the memory processes that are involved. To illustrate, the flow of information during learning is acted on by the sensory memory which only lasts about .5 seconds, thereafter, is moved to the working memory, which may retain it for only 20-30 seconds before it is stored in the long term memory for retrieval and recall at a later time (Driscoll, 2005). Thus, in order to optimize recall and retrieval of information, encoding strategies are performed when the information is in the working memory before it can be moved to the long term memory. Once the information is in the long term memory, again strategies are employed in order to be able to retrieve it upon demand. The information is stored in a form called schema which is a "data structure for representing the generic concepts stored in the memory" (Driscoll, 2005, p. 129).

Constructivism.

Many have echoed in the educational arena that "constructivism stands out as one much heralded alternative that has been widely promoted in recent times in attempts at moving away from the old ways of instruction and their attendant limitations" (Kumar, 2006, p. 247). "Constructivist theory rests on the assumption that knowledge is constructed by learners as they attempt to make sense of their experiences...constructive processes operate and learners form, elaborate, and test candidate mental structures until a satisfactory one emerges" (Driscoll, 2005, p. 387).

Driscoll (2005) and Dijkstra et al. (1997) have stated with conviction that there is no single constructivist theory when it comes to learning and instruction. The learning conditions for constructivist teachings emphasize the "process of learning," much like Gagné's (1985) versus Reigeluth's (1999) conditions of learning which emphasize "how to teach." Driscoll adequately summarized the constructivist conditions of learning as:

> (a) embed learning in complex, realistic, and relevant environments; (b) provide for social negotiation as an integral part of learning; (c) support multiple perspectives and the use of multiple modes of representations; (d) encourage ownership in learning; and (e) nurture self-awareness of the knowledge construction process. (pp. 393-394)

Constructivists do not subscribe to learning objectives that are too structured, believing that the learner loses the ability to make meaning of them in relationship to the real world context they are supposed to support. However, they do believe in learning goals when formed in context with meaningful activity and when the learner identifies and pursues their own learning goals (Driscoll, 2005). The constructivist goals are the "ability to solve ill-structured problems (Jonassen & Land, 2000), acquire content knowledge from complex domains along with critical thinking and collaboration skills (Nelson, 1999), develop personal acquisition skills (Hannafin, Land, & Oliver, 1999)" (Driscoll, 2005, p. 391), and "use multiple modes of representation to identify knowledge in different ways" (Driscoll, 2005, p. 394). These goals confirm the constructivist philosophy that "knowledge does not come into its own until the learner can deploy it with understanding" (Perkins & Unger, 1999, p. 94).

Constructivists believe that the student's motivation to learn is activated by involving them in meaningful, relevant activities that spur their interest and excitement. "Students in a learning experience that is truly constructive should find themselves swept up in activities that they find meaningful....progress and develop at a pace uniquely appropriate for them....learning experiences are interdisciplinary and not restricted to subject matter" (Knight, 2002, p. 8). Further, "using constructivist theory as a foundation for assessment design suggests a greater emphasis on cognitive processing (versus content topics or visible behaviors) as assessments are designed" (Zane, 2009).

Points of convergence between cognitive systems approach to course development and the constructive approach to course development.

There are points of convergence between the two approaches, especially within the teaching realm. In constructivist learning, even though the instructor is relegated to act as a mediator, this does not preclude them from using strategies such as scaffolding to assist the students' development within their zone of proximal development (Knight, 2002). In the systems approach, scaffolding plays an important role in ensuring that the information is mastered before moving to the next level of content.

The conditions of learning for both constructivist theory and the systems approach utilize many of the same learning theories (as you will study in Chapter 4). Schema theory, mental models, situated cognition, social learning theory, multiple intelligence, cognitive flexibility theory, collaborative learning, and problem scaffolding are integral to the systems approach by Gagné (1985) and Reigeluth (1999). Not only do the approaches utilize the same theories, but also many of the same instructional strategies to ensure retention and transfer of learning.

Although the extremists of each approach to the best instructional design may believe they are at odds and cannot be compatible in a learning environment, Reigeluth (1999) contended these two theories offer different perspectives on the learning process and to reject one for the other would be "nonconstructivist....I prefer to think of them as complementary design tools....to be applied in different contexts" (p. 10). He is not alone in this view for Morrison et al. (2004), Simpson (2002), and Smith and Ragan (1999) also proposed constructivist strategies as well as cognitive and prescriptive strategies be considered in course development.

Therefore, it would seem that the best type of instructional methodology to promote teaching and learning in the design of instruction would be a combination of the systems approach and to infuse constructivist strategies.

Development Techniques.

Do not forget the reason you are developing the instruction; you must address a specific problem. You already developed objectives to address the problem so the instructional strategies you include throughout the instruction needs to support mastery of those objectives by the learner. In reflecting back to the learner analysis, you should have discovered (1) the reading level of the learner or audience, (2) any prior knowledge the learner has on the subject and (3) the learner or audience's background that will affect the appropriate context for examples that will be included in the instruction. Clark and Mayer (2011) are well known for their work in designing instruction. Some instruction techniques that have proven to enhance learning and retention of the information are:

1. Apply the Multimedia Principle: "Multimedia representations can encourage learners to engage in active learning by mentally representing the material in words and in pictures and by mentally making connections between the pictorial and verbal representations" (Clark & Mayer, 2011, p. 71);

2. Select graphics that support learning. Clark and Mayer (2011) describe 5 different types of graphics but only recommend graphics that are (1) transformational or interpretive that assists the learner to understand the material, and (2) organize the information for the learner (p. 71);

3. Apply the Contiguity Principle: Align words to corresponding graphics (in the same space or contiguous) and audio should be heard at the same time the learner views the corresponding graphic or animation;

4. Apply the Modality Principle: Present words as audio narration rather than on screen text (Clark & Mayer, 2011, p. 115). According to the cognitive theory of learning, people process information in 2 separate channels: visual/pictorial and auditory/verbal processing. The capacity of each channel is limited; therefore one's ability to simultaneously look at the graphics and read the text impairs their learning and retention of the information.

5. Apply the Redundancy Principle: On screen text provided with narrated graphics is considered redundant. When this happens the learner is conflicted between reading the text, looking at the graphic, and reconciling the audio with the actual text on the screen. The cognitive processing becomes overloaded thus hindering the learning process;

6. Apply the Coherence Principle: Keep the lesson simple. Avoid adding anything (graphics, audio, animation, simpler visuals, etc.) that does NOT support the instructional goal;

7. Apply the Personalization Principle: Instruction should be written in the conversational style. "Research on discourse processing shows that people work harder to understand material when they feel they are in

conversation with a partner, rather than simply receiving information" (Clark & Mayer, 2011, p. 184); and

8. Apply the Segmenting and Pre-training Principles: When the material is complex, you break the information into segments for better learning and retention. Mayer and Chandler in 2001, carried out a study where they found that the learners who received segmented presentations on a subject performed better on transfer tests than the learners who received a continuous presentation, even though the information was identical. This idea supports the Gagne and Reigeluth principles of designing instruction in a building block format that links one piece of information to another in the learning process. The Pre-training Principle focuses on introducing the learner to key concepts, names of parts, or characteristics of the subject to be studied prior to the start of the lesson or course. By using an orientation session or incorporating into advance organizers, learners are more able to understand and retain the information when they can connect the key concepts or names with the content.

Creating the Environment for Learning.

Creating an environment for learning is just as important as it is to develop instructional strategies that will promote learning and retention of information. These conditions can be directly correlated to Gagné and Reigeluth's good learning practices. Gagné (1985) specifies these conditions as:

1. Gaining the attention of the student with various methods of presenting the new information;
2. Informing the learner of the objective so there is an understanding of why they are learning this new information;
3. Stimulating the recall of prior learning through various instructional techniques so they can see why the new information has relevance;
4. Presenting the stimulus because every type of learning requires some type of stimulus. "The stimulus presented as an instructional event depends on specifically what is to be learned" (p. 252);
5. Providing learning guidance which supports the semantic encoding internal process making the stimulus meaningful and relevant;
6. Eliciting performance whereby the learner now is required to demonstrate in some fashion, the newly learned capability;
7. Providing feedback to the learner to ensure they understand the correct way to perform the new capability; and
8. Assessing the learner's performance to ensure that the instruction has been learned and retained.

Implementation of the Instruction and Evaluation.

The implementation phase is used to deliver the instructions to the learner; the evaluation phase determines if the instructional objectives have been achieved. The evaluation phase should be used throughout the entire instructional design process, within phases, between phases, and after implementation (McGriff, 2001).

As you are designing the instruction, the Formative Evaluation phase begins simultaneously. Formative evaluation is used to provide feedback to the designer at the start of the ID process and continue through the completion of the course. There are several phases of the formative evaluation: (1) design reviews which take place as each phase of the design is completed, i.e., the establishment of the goals, learner and contextual analysis, task analysis, design of the course and actual development of the materials. "This design review serves to ensure the accuracy of each phase" (Smith & Ragan, 1999, p. 339); (2) expert reviews are used to ensure that the instructional materials and the content reflect accurately the learning goals and objectives already defined; (3) learner validation is much like a "trial" before implementation to actual learners to determine if there are any pitfalls in the design of the instruction; and finally, the ongoing evaluation where the designer collects and analyzes the data collected throughout the other formative phases. The last two phases are normally conducted with a group much like the target audience, but not the target audience.

The Summative Evaluation is to collect, analyze, and summarize the data through assessments given to your target audience at the end of the instruction. The results of the assessment data will allow you to determine the effectiveness and efficiency of the instruction, and if the instruction met the goals you defined in the very beginning of this undertaking. If you are a designer employed by an agency or organization to resolve an identified training problem, this data can be used to determine if the instruction should be continued or that it really does NOT resolve their problem, and another course of action must be taken. Remember, this was the initial reason why a specific instruction was envisioned in the first place. If the instruction does NOT resolve the problem, it could be that the instruction was not required in the first place. Hopefully, through the analysis phases of identifying the problem, this would have been ascertained.

The types of assessment instruments that can be used in the Summative Evaluation phase are identified in Chapter 5 of this handbook.

EMERGENT ID MODELS

We cannot leave this chapter without addressing there are constantly new theories and models devised annually by the scholars in the ID discipline. This handbook was not devised to try to capture all that have been published. However, there are two models that seem to be popular with those who are now teaching ID so you should be aware of them.

The first is the ***ASSURE ID Model***. ASSURE is the acronym for (1) Analyze the learners (2) State standards and objectives, (3) Select strategies, technology, media, and materials, (4) Utilize technology, media, and materials, (5) Require learner participation, and (6) Evaluate and revise. As the ADDIE Model is a basic model for the ID process, the ASSURE Model uses a step-by-step process that effectively integrates the use of technology and media throughout the curriculum. The ASSURE Model directly aligns with the National Education Technology Standards for Teachers as well as curriculum standards from the local and national level (Baran, 2010).

The components of an instructional plan are used to build a well-structured plan that includes all aspects of a number of instructional design models. However, an instructional plan is useless without an effective plan of implementation that delivers the instruction so that objectives are met. The purposes of instructional design models are to help design instructional plans that are effective in achieving the learning objectives.

Another popular instructional design is called the ***Backward Design***. The design is based on the premise that the assessment is devised first. You should know what you want the final outcome to be before you design your instruction to meet that goal. Made notable by Wiggins and McTighe (2011), the Backward Design is being practiced by many instructional designers now. This design focuses on 3 specific tasks: (1) Identifying the desired results by streamlining "what is critical to learn". What is important for the learner to take away from this material? (2) Determining acceptable evidence that will prove that the learner actually "learned" what your instruction was designed for them to learn. Sounds very simple but many times instructors teach what they THINK the learner should know. (3) The last stage is plan the learning instruction. Sounds like the first stage of the ADDIE, right?

This course was designed in a Backward Design thought process. We knew the jobs that exist for this type of knowledge base (course design), so we selected the particular specific areas within those jobs keeping in mind, *"what is critical for the learner to take away from this instruction."* Then we designed the handbook and the curriculum to include *only those critical areas of study.* The last portion of this curriculum was to now concentrate on the design within the *actual syllabi, select the faculty, and design the activities* that will support the learning outcomes in each segment of the instruction.

CHAPTER 3

ADULT LEARNING AND TECHNOLOGY

Current research supports the notion that "discovery-oriented learning *environments* are essential for the development and effective transfer of higher-order skills applied in critical thinking, discourse, and problem-solving" (Visser, Visser, & Scholosser, 2003, p. 5). Because the learning populace across the nation are adult learners, it would seem prudent to consider a more dynamic approach to learning as advocated by Knowles (1970, 1984, 1990; Knowles, Holton, & Swanson, 2011), referred to as the andragogical method to learning.

Andragogy. To define Andragogy as a learning theory has met with some controversy; therefore, Knowles (1984) has defined it as a "set of concepts" (p. 8) and promotes it as a model or process design to learning. Andragogy is tailored to the specific differences one encounters when teaching adult learners. Andragogical principles embrace the strategies that promote critical thinking. Knowles (1990) advocates self-directed learning whereby the learner is in control of what is to be learned and how it is learned.

Andragogy is built on the following assumptions (Knowles, 1990):

1. "Adults need to know why they need to learn something before undertaking to learn it" (p. 57);
2. "Adults have a self-concept of being responsible for their own decisions, for their own lives" (p. 58). When adults enter an educational environment, they tend to resort back to their conditioning from past school experiences, and become a passive learner;
3. The learner's experience becomes crucial to further learning, thus providing the schema to build future, expansive knowledge structures. As Knowles notes, "for many kinds of learning, the richest resources for learning reside in the adult learners themselves" (p. 59). Because our experiences denote who we are, any situation whereby those experiences are not valued or ignored becomes interpreted by the adult learner as a rejection of him/her as a contributor to the learning experience;
4. Adults show a readiness to learn when they pursue education in order to deal with real-life situations. Knowles promotes inducements such as simulations which assists the adult learner in their readiness to progress;

5. Adults are life-centered, therefore their orientation to learning is task or problem-centered, whereby they must utilize critical thinking skills in the context of real-life situations. They learn more effectively when they can apply the new knowledge to their everyday lives; and

6. Adult motivation factors center on external motivators, such as promotion, and increased job satisfaction. However, barriers, such as a negative self-concept as a student, time constraints, and life events, impact accessibility to education. Thus, if the principles of adult learning are not addressed in the design of education for this group of learners, their goals may never be realized. (Knowles, 1990)

Learning theories are of little use unless "they are applied somehow to the facilitation of learning...presumably the learning theory subscribed to by a teacher will influence [his] theory of teaching" (p. 66). As Knowles (1990) and Gagné (1985) advocate, conditions for learning must be present to facilitate the learning process. The eight conditions of learning merge internal and external processes together in a learning situation. Internal conditions are schema structured from the individual's life experiences, versus external events which influence internal processes and enhance the learning process (Gagné, 1985).

There has also been research on applying brain-based strategies in combination with adult learning principles to make education more effective (Trapp, 2005). Using color, graphics, and positive language set the stage for learning; humor, and self-directed learning formats that incorporate the use of multiple senses, can capitalize on how the brain absorbs and stores information (Trapp, 2005). These strategies complement the principles set forth by Gagné (1985) and Knowles (1990) when devising instruction for adult learners.

Knowles (1990) asserted when dealing with adult learners, the conditions of learning should include the following: (a) Provide an environment whereby the learners feel a need to learn by exposing students to the objective, helping the student "diagnose the gap between his aspiration and his present level of performance" (p. 85) and assist the student in identifying the problems encountered in their own lives when that gap is present; (b) create a learning environment that is "characterized by physical comfort, mutual trust and respect, mutual helpfulness, freedom of expression, and acceptance of differences" (p. 85). As with Gagné's (1985) conditions of learning, Knowles (1984) also stressed the need to design the right physical environment as well as a conducive psychological environment for learning. This psychological environment is just as important to learning as the physical environment and has seven specific characteristics: "(a) a climate of mutual respect, (b) a climate of collaborativeness, (c) a climate of mutual trust, (d) a climate of supportiveness, (e) a climate of openness and authenticity, (f) a climate of pleasure, and (g) a climate of humanness" (pp. 15-17). With these elements present, the learning process becomes relevant and the life experience of the learner becomes critical in the learning process.

The elements described above are part of the process design of the andragogical model. When applied, this model or process is considered a better educational teaching method for specific subject topics such as "problem solving, cultural diversity, sexual harassment, conflict resolution, interpersonal communication skills, and community organization skills" (Birzer & Tannehill, 2001, p. 241).

Focusing on developing a person's critical thinking skills are at the forefront of designing instruction for today's environment. Critical thinking has been deemed as one of the aspects within the 21st century skill set needed to operate and compete in the business world of today. Critical thinking is a learner's ability to demonstrate a strong ability to compare, contrast, interpret, analyze, and synthesize concepts and ideas. Therefore, when designing course instruction, you must communicate instructions and assignments that seek to develop specific thinking skills such as those detailed by Bloom's taxonomy: evaluation, synthesis, analysis, application, comprehension, and knowledge.

Evaluation and differentiation teaches the learner how to compare and discriminate, access statements and arguments, looks for evidence to support assumptions and beliefs, and is able to clearly define a set of criteria for analyzing ideas. Using higher level of Bloom's taxonomy ensures the learner gathers enough knowledge in which they demonstrate they grasped a concept. We believe the responsibility for learning rests not only with the student, but with the instructor therefore, learning should be the focus of everything we do. When we create course assignments we must provide detailed instructions and assignments in order for learners to develop a higher level of thinking.

The process of learning has been enumerated by many seminal theorists such as Skinner (1974), Piaget (1971), and Vygotsky (1978). Each has focused on the developmental aspects of how we learn and process information from infancy to adulthood. Chapter 4 outlines the seminal theorists and those specific theories that deal with the educational psychology of learning. An instructional designer can only devise instruction efficiently and effectively if you understand these theories.

CHAPTER 4

EDUCATIONAL PSYCHOLOGY

Educational psychology incorporates a number of other disciplines: developmental psychology, behavioral psychology, and cognitive psychology. The learning process of early childhood and adolescence impacts the way individuals learn at later stages in life. Not only are these determinants of how people learn, but our social, emotional, and cognitive processes that can be identified throughout an entire lifespan, can impact the way we learn. Therefore, in this chapter we will address the theories behind developmental psychology, behavioral psychology and cognitive psychology.

Development Psychology

a. The Psychoanalytic Theory. Psychoanalytic theory was originated by Sigmund Freud. He believed that childhood experiences and unconscious desires influenced behavior, thus developing a theory that proposed that development occurred in stages and the conflicts that occur during each of these stages can have a lifelong influence on personality and behavior. Seen as one of the most controversial theories in psychology, Freud advocated that personality developed in the childhood stages whereby satisfaction of the "pleasure seeking energies" (id) must be satisfied to result in a healthy personality in later years.

According to Cherry (2013), "Psychoanalytic theory suggested that personality is mostly established by the age of five. Early experiences play a large role in personality development and continue to influence behavior later in life" (para. 4). If certain issues are not resolved at the appropriate stage, a persistent focus or fixation occurs, and the individual could remain in one stage indefinitely. "For example, a person who is fixated at the oral stage may be over-dependent on others and may seek oral stimulation through smoking, drinking, or eating" (Cherry, 2013, para. 5).

b. Psychosocial Development: Erik Erikson's theory of psychosocial

development is one of the best-known theories of personality in psychology, focusing on the impact of one's social experiences across their lifespan (Cô & Levine, 1988). One of the main elements of the theory concentrates on the development of what is called an **ego identity.** An identity consists of the beliefs, ideals, and values that help shape and guide a person's behavior, beginning in the childhood years and extending through one's lifetime. Erikson also believed that a sense of competence motivates one's behaviors and actions, therefore at each stage one is concerned with becoming competent in an area of life. If the stage is handled well, the person will feel a sense of mastery, which is sometimes referred to as **ego strength** or **ego quality**. If the stage is managed poorly, the person will emerge with a sense of inadequacy. Thus these stages are as follows:

- **Psychosocial Stage 1 - Trust vs. Mistrust (birth to age 1).** The infant is totally dependent and the development of trust is based on the care or neglect given at this time by others in the child's life. If the child feels safe and secure, trust will be instilled. If these conditions do not occur at this stage, the child could fail to develop trust thus resulting in fear and a belief that the world is inconsistent and unpredictable. This fear can manifest itself into trust issues in later life.

- **Psychosocial Stage 2 - Autonomy vs. Shame and Doubt (age 2-3 years).** Vander Zanden (2003) contended, "As children become mobile, they must decide whether to assert their wills. Favored outcome: A sense of self control without a loss of self-esteem" (p. 43). Important events that occur at this stage are their control over food choice, toy selection, and clothing selection, to name a few.

- **Psychosocial Stage 3 - Initiative vs. Guilt (age 4-5 years).** Cherry (2013) claimed, "During the preschool years, children begin to assert their power and control over the world through directing play and other social interactions. Children who are successful at this stage feel capable and able to lead others. Those who fail to acquire these skills are left with a sense of guilt, self-doubt, and lack of initiative" (para. 18).

- **Psychosocial Stage 4 - Industry vs. Inferiority** (age 6-12 years). At this stage children begin to focus on how things work and are made. Through their social interactions, a sense of pride in their accomplishments and abilities begins to develop. Those who are encouraged and commended on what they have accomplished will develop a feeling of competence and belief in their skills. Those who receive little or no encouragement will doubt their abilities to be successful.
- **Psychosocial Stage 5 - Identity vs. Confusion (13–24 years).** Prior to this stage, encouragement and reinforcement would set the stage for individuals to emerge with a strong sense of self and a feeling of independence and control. Those who remain unsure of their beliefs and desires will feel insecure and confused about themselves and the future.
- **Psychosocial Stage 6 – Intimacy vs. Isolation (young adulthood).** This stage focused on the individual's ability to reach out and make contact with others. The positive feedback in this stage would allow one to work towards a career and find intimacy with others.
- **Psychosocial Stage 7 – Generativity vs. Stagnation (adulthood).** At this stage one looks beyond oneself embracing society, service to others and the future.

The last 2 stages deal with old age from the years 60+. Since these do not impact the learning stages that we are discussing in this book, we will not address them here.

Behavior Psychology

Behaviorism. Behaviorism is based on the premise that "learning can be fully understood in terms of observable events, both behavioral and environmental" (Driscoll, 2005, p. 6). This school of thought was founded by John B. Watson and expanded on by B. F. Skinner who believed that "behavior could be fully understood in terms of environmental cues and results" (p. 33). The following are the learning processes advocated under Behaviorism.

a. Classical Conditioning, according to Cherry (2005), "is a learning process in which an association is made between a previously neutral stimulus and a stimulus that naturally evokes a response. For example, in Pavlov's classic experiment, the smell of food was the naturally occurring stimulus that was paired with the previously neutral ringing of the bell. Once an association had been made between the two, the sound of the bell alone could lead to a response" (para. 1).

b. Operant conditioning is a learning process whereby the response is based on increased or decreased rewards or punishments. One will act based on the expectation that they will receive something in return.

c. Observational Learning is when learning occurs by observing and imitating others (also known as modeling). Albert Bandura's (1977) classic "Bobo Doll" experiments confirmed that individuals will imitate the actions of others without direct reinforcement.

Cognitive Psychology

Cognitive theory is concerned with the development of a person's thought processes. The foremost scholar in this area was Jean Piaget, who proposed a theory that included 4 distinct stages in a child's intellectual development:

a. *the sensorimotor stage, from birth to age 2* whereby the child becomes goal-oriented in behavior;

b. *the preoperational stage, from age 2 to about age 7.* The child at this stage engages in symbolic play and language games and has difficulty with more than one view of a problem or solution.

c. *the concrete operational stage, from age 7 to 11.* The child performs mental observations and can solve concrete problems but has difficulty in thinking hypothetically about a problem.

d. *the formal operational stage, which begins in adolescence and spans into adulthood.* This is the stage where the child has progressed to solving abstract problems, thinks hypothetically and develops concerns over social issues.

Piaget suggested that the change in the child through the stages is *qualitative, i.e., the change occurs in how they thinks about the world. Some of the important concepts introduced by Piaget have had a tremendous* impact on education. Many educational programs are now built upon the belief that children should be taught at the level for which they are developmentally prepared. In addition to this, a number of instructional strategies have been derived from Piaget's work. These strategies include providing a supportive environment, utilizing social interactions and peer teaching, and helping children see fallacies and inconsistencies in their thinking (Driscoll, 2000).

Some key concepts derived from Piaget and are used today to explain learning and retention of information are:

Schemas – Clark (1999) purported, "Information is stored in a form called schema. Data of 2 types are included in schemata: (1) declarative which is information about things and (2) procedural which is information on how to do things" (p. 13). An example would be if a child has a stuffed animal (puppy) which is the only thing in the house that is called a puppy, then the child believes that this is a puppy. But when the child is actually introduced to a real puppy, then the schema is modified to include this new information.

Assimilation – This occurs when we take in new information into our previously existing schemas. For example, when one learns a new skill such as a new app on their phones, they tend to apply that knowledge in as many situations as possible.

Accommodation - "When existing schemes or operations must be modified to account for the new experience" (Clark, 1999, p. 198).

Equilibration – This is the master development process which encompasses maintaining a balance between applying previous knowledge (assimilation) and changing behavior to account for new knowledge (accommodation) (Driscoll, 2000, p. 199).

Social Learning Theory

Devised by Bandura (1977), it is based on the belief that direct reinforcement could not account for all types of learning. "The social learning theory distinguishes between acquisition and performance because people do not enact everything they learn. They are more likely to adopt modeled behavior if it results in outcomes they value that if it has unrewarding or punishing effects" (p. 28). In other words, just because something has been learned, it does not mean that it will result in a change in behavior.

Socio-Cultural Theory

Vygotsky (1978) is credited with this theory premised on:

(1) Development will differ depending on when and where you grow up;

(2) Development will also be effected when you have a change in a social situation or what activities one undertakes;

(3) "Activities are usually done in groups during social interaction" (Vander Zanden, 2003, p. 51);

(4) Persons will observe an activity, and then internalize it with the use of signs and symbols such as language; and

(5) By interacting with other cultures, one can assimilate the values of that culture.

Constructivist Theory

Scholars and educators have started embracing the constructivist point of view, criticizing and advocating abandonment of the systems approach (Dijkstra, Schott, Seel, & Tennyson, 1997; Duffy & Kirkley, 2004; Jonassen & Land, 2000). Constructivism proposed that the best learning and transfer of knowledge happens when learners create their own knowledge based on what they already know. In support of constructivism, current research supports the notion that discovery-oriented learning environments are essential for the development and effective transfer of higher-order skills applied in critical thinking, discourse, and problem-solving (Visser, Visser, & Schlosser, 2003).

Constructivist origins started as early as 1916 with educational reformer, John Dewey, who posited that social interaction promotes learning by integrating knowledge with life experiences (McAninch, 2006). For the advocates of constructivism, Jean Piaget's theories on child development and their mental processes for learning, has become the foundation for this educational movement (Iran-Nejad, 1995). There are numerous theorists who articulate various aspects of the constructivist theory as evidenced by the following: discovery learning by Bruner (Driscoll, 2000), generative learning by Wittrock (1989), cognitive flexibility theory by Spiro, Coulson, Feltovich, and Anderson (1988), case-based reasoning by Shank, Berman, and Macpherson (1999), situated cognition theory by Clancey (Driscoll, 2000), problem-centered learning and inquiry-based learning by Duffy and Kirkley (2004).

These are only a select few and to name all of the theories that purport to be constructivist would extend the length of this chapter dramatically. Therefore, those theories enumerated above should provide a general, but full understanding of the constructivism learning theory movement.

The last section to be addressed that impacts learning and thus the design of instruction for learners, is the individual's learning style or preference. A learning style refers to the best way you seem to learn and process new information. Each of us has our own unique way of learning. There are three main learning styles.

Visual Learning Style

Visual learners learn primarily through seeing and tend to learn best using visual aids such as illustrations, diagrams and charts. Listening to a lecture without visual cues can be difficult for visual learners. Many visual learners also find that taking notes to read through later can help them to remember information.

Auditory Learning Style

Auditory learners learn primarily through hearing. They learn best by listening to lectures and discussing information. These students tend to have strong language and oral-communication skills, and often have innate musical abilities as well. They may have trouble processing written information; however, they can benefit greatly by reading information aloud, or by having information read to them.

Kinesthetic Learning Style

Kinesthetic learners learn primarily through touching, doing, and moving. They learn best by experiencing things. Kinesthetic students thrive when given the opportunity to do hands-on experiments. They tend to have difficulty sitting still for long periods, and need to get up and move frequently. "Educational tools such as manipulatives, hands-on models and field trips can greatly benefit this type of learner" (Cheever, 2013, p. 1).

Why is it important to understand that your learners have different learning styles? Spiro and his colleagues (1995) advocated the use of multiple forms of models and multiple representations of the same information for maximum retention and understanding of information that is presented. "Using multiple modes of representation can serve as a means of juxtaposition. That is, viewing the same content through different sensory modes (such as visual, auditory, or tactile) again enables different aspects of it to be seen" (Driscoll, 2000, p. 399). Most of us learn though a combination of these three learning styles, but one style is usually dominant. For these reasons, the best instructional design is to ensure that you have included activities that "draw in" all types of learners, thus learning the content from many different modes.

CHAPTER 5

ASSESSMENT AND EVALUATION OF ACADEMIC PERFORMANCE

Learning is a continuous process that can take place anywhere at any time and extends throughout a lifetime. Learning is the process of acquiring knowledge and abilities through example, abstract thinking, experimentation, and the teaching of others. This process of learning involves the acquisition of knowledge, the improved ability to think rationally, and developing emotional maturity. Learning is done through inquiry, experimentation, and abstract thinking. One of the main objectives of learning is to acquire knowledge and new skills; however, one cannot know if learning has occurred without appropriate assessment. The appropriate assessment should not only be carried out on the learners but also to their teachers in order for them to gauge whether they are effectively teaching.

Valid assessment is crucial as it helps to identify instructional needs...and for instructors to devise teaching plans (Ku, 2009, p. 71). Additionally, as per the Delphi Report (Facione, 1990), the recommendations identified in regards to assessments, focuses on not *what* assessment instruments are preferred but on what a good assessment should include as construct properties, i.e., "content validity, construct validity, reliability and fairness" (pp. 15-16).

An Action Plan for Achievement Tests and Performance Tests

People often think the main role of assessment is to provide judgment on the performance of the school in relation to educational reforms; however, assessment is a formal attempt to determine students' status with respect to educational variables of interest and increase engagement. Since the late twentieth century, educators use assessment to inform instruction, gather data about what students know prior to beginning instruction, gather data about how well students are understanding during instruction, and adjust instruction and reteach when necessary in an effort to ensure that all students can be successful in the end. Teachers therefore, have to use a wide variety of assessments to assist them in making instructional decisions that are appropriate and valid for a variety of diverse learners (Bartunek, 2007).

Information from assessments is designed to increase student achievement and accomplish the following goals: motivate students to want to do better, give students useful information they can use to do better, and inform teachers' reteaching plans so students can do better. Assessment information is also used for accountability reporting to parents, communities, and other various levels. Prior to implementing the intervention plan, the teacher must articulate lessons and unit objectives that are worth learning, shares with students what the objectives are and why they are worth learning, and clarifies them daily for students in a form comparable with statements such as "You (students) will demonstrate that you are able to ... by ..." This process gives students something to aim at and the teachers an idea for evaluating the learning experiences. The goal of this intervention is to positively impact student achievement. Therefore, failing to collect data on student achievement would be a major mistake, one that could hinder a school's reform effort (Barki & Pinsonneault as cited in Johnson, 2010). In this step, teachers would be charged with identifying any areas with student learning issues. After they identify learning concerns, they would be encouraged to consult with each other and come up with methods other than state and standardized tests that could be used to address the problems found. Teachers deal directly with learners and know most of their needs; therefore, they are the best source to provide adequate information about student achievement. The learner would inform teachers that there are other ways of collecting evidence regarding the impact of interventions on student achievement besides state tests and standardized tests (Barki & Pinsonneault as cited in Johnson, 2010).

The learner would introduce methods such as remedial classes, through which the areas that have been identified as having problems would be revisited or re-taught through a program organized by the teachers. Incentives to motivate teachers to dedicate their time to these remedial classes would be offered. Problematic subjects would receive an extra period, and targeted services and special assistance would be given to students who have disabilities in learning or any other special needs (Cummings, Maddux, & Richmond as cited in Johnson, 2010). Classes would contain a diverse student population, and based on the results of achievement tests, teachers would be encouraged to expand the learning options for learners, which would allow them to reach the highest standards. This could be done through flexible and creative scheduling in learning and instruction to create an extension of learning time for students who might require it (Perie, Marion, & Gong as cited in Johnson, 2010). Teachers would be encouraged to engage students in one-on-one tutoring or cross-age tutoring with older students to address specific student needs.

Curricula would be developed that offers coursework that is challenging to develop high-achieving students. Research has proven that giving easier assignments or simpler lessons does not solve poor performance problems, providing no assurance that students will perform better (Pearson as cited in Johnson, 2010). Therefore, the learner would advocate for challenging assignments that are intellectually stimulating to create a learning environment that is high-achieving. Teachers would use their skills exhaustively to provide instruction and meaningful assignments while holding high expectations for students (Pearson as cited in Johnson, 2010). Such assignments would address significant concepts in the diverse disciplines, incorporating skills that promote critical thinking while they relate concepts to the real world. The learner would also promote computer-based testing because electronic surveys or questionnaires are an efficient tool for collecting information about students' backgrounds, prior experiences, interests, and beliefs (Airasian & Russell as cited in Johnson, 2010).

The world is developing at a very rapid rate, and so is the information technology field. Much schoolwork is conducted digitally. This has made it easier for various learning institutions to integrate and share their views as well as their examinations. Due to this technological advancement, the school should incorporate computer-based examinations, which will update the students with other extra curriculum activities and expand their ability to be innovative (Zammuto, Griffith, Majchrzak, Dougherty, & Faraj as cited in Johnson, 2010). Additionally, there are many references posted on scholarly Websites that can be of great help to students as research tools in their studies. Students should also be given online tests, which are not internally set, to broaden their learning perspectives. If students are successful with these tests, it is an indication that it was a good performance assessment. Discussion times that last for substantial periods would be introduced to encourage the sharing of ideas among students (Zepke & Leach as cited in Johnson, 2010).

Teaching decisions and classroom instruction will be guided through ongoing assessment-based performance since this would ensure that no learning problem goes unnoticed and the problems would, thus, be addressed as they emerge (Cornelius-White as cited in Johnson, 2010). Assessment would be made continuously and consistently throughout the year in order for teachers to get detailed information on the academic progress of the students with regard to how much they know their capabilities, their learning styles, and their problematic areas. This would ensure that all of their instructional needs are met. The use of performance assessments and achievement test tools best inform teaching and act as instructional guides. Assessment based on performance is the best reflection of new instruction methods and standards of education (Cornelius-White as cited in Johnson, 2010).

The use of performance assessment results to identify struggling learners, especially in lower grades, will guide the learner in hiring specialists to work with teachers in helping to address these student needs. Highly trained teachers would also be hired to provide intervention programs for at-risk. Teachers and learners would be grouped together for longer periods through the creation of family groups where students of mixed performance are grouped together and assigned a patron (Pearson as cited in Johnson, 2010). The groups would act as families in helping each other to solve personal and academic problems. This could also occur through multiage grouping, looping, or grouping in teams.

In every learning institution, teachers often use assessments to provide feedback that will help them to improve their teaching to meet the instructional needs of students. The feedback obtained helps teachers to bridge gaps that might be present between student achievement and curriculum standards. Assessment tests are also used for the purpose of accountability in regard to teachers and students. The learner's plan would include frequent and early intervention programs that identify those who need special attention and provide many alternatives so they can receive support. This would only be possible through the use of diagnostic and ongoing assessments of teachers to allow the development of intervention strategies to help intercept learners who are unable to adapt while accelerating learning.

Three widely used assessment instruments, e.g., student evaluations, rubrics, and pre-tests/post-tests, are normally designed as a multiple-choice test with some open-ended questions to expand on the response. According to Benjamin (2008), President of the Council for Aid to Education (CAE), "Most standardized testing is still based on multiple-choice and short answer formats...the current testing regime is not assessing the most critical skills required of students in the workplace..." (p. 4). These assessments take a "multidimensional "construct" ...and try to break it down into its component parts- critical thinking, analytic reasoning, and communication. Then individual test items, subtests or tests are constructed to tap each component. Finally the components are put back together again to provide a total score (Klein, Benjamin, Shavelson, & Bolus, 2007, p. 6).

This "construct" approach is based on the premise that each component can be measured or scored individually, thus each "critical thinking skill can be evaluated separately. By putting all the parts back together one can then see an entire picture" (Klein et al., 2007, p. 6). The disadvantage is "that it is often artificial and neglects the fact that the whole is usually much greater than the sum of its parts" (p. 6). The dissection loses much in the translation and also loses pieces when trying to put all the parts back together. Klein et al., (2007) uses the analogy of learning to drive a car safely: one may know the rules of the road by being able to read all the gauges but that does not mean one can drive the car safely.

The selection of the proper assessment instrument is crucial in order to ascertain whether the learners actually acquired higher-order, critical thinking skills from the instruction presented. If the end result is not assessed by the proper instrument, then nothing substantial may be known about what was learned. A common starting technique in the assessment of student achievement is a Background Knowledge Probe, a term that refers to the use of short questionnaires prepared by teachers at the beginning of a new unit or lesson (Rupp & Lesaux as cited in Johnson, 2010). This probe serves the purpose of a relevant starting point in order to begin new instruction. The probe's results allows for adequate focus on the part of the students, as the teachers will know which material to teach before moving to a new lesson.

Another introductory technique is focused listing, whereby students concentrate on finding significant terms and concepts from lessons and then list ideas they consider closely associated with a given focus point (Vitullo & Jones as cited in Johnson, 2010). In this way, teachers help students to recall important information on a particular issue so that they can further apply the mastered concepts in practice.

In the process of providing adequate educational assessment, teachers can also rely on the benefits of formative assessment, which is perceived as a promising way to enhance student motivation and achievement (Hassett & Curwood as cited in Johnson, 2010). Formative assessment is a continuous process dominated by collecting assessment-elicited evidence of student learning. Then, educators modify instruction in a precise response to feedback. A helpful way of understanding the relevance of formative assessment is to contrast it with summative assessment. The latter is concerned solely with recording current student achievement. Summative assessment is an assessment at the end of a period of education or training that sums up how a student has performed (Airasian & Russell as cited in Johnson, 2010). An example of summative assessment is a post-test given in algebra, reading comprehension, or keyboarding to determine mastery of objectives. Even though formative assessment can be used after a test, teachers utilize this type of assessment during instruction so that they can identify misunderstandings and help students to correct their errors. Ongoing formative assessment is mainly conducted through informal observations and oral questions (Kennedy & Shiel Pearson as cited in Johnson, 2010).

Formative assessment measures several points during a teaching/learning phase, with the primary intention of obtaining information to guide further teaching or learning steps. Formative assessments include questioning, comments on a presentation, or interviewing (Airasian & Russell as cited in Johnson, 2010). An example of formative assessment is a pretest given in an academic area such as algebra, reading comprehension, or keyboarding skills. The teacher would drive the instructional strategy and the development of lesson plans with this information. As they are closely related to the approaches of systems thinking and system dynamics, formative assessment can be considered as a set of characteristics that are present in any situation. In other words, some assessment procedures may only demonstrate evidence of student performance and feedback, whereas others illustrate the use of more characteristics (Airasian & Russell as cited in Johnson, 2010). Nevertheless, formative and summative data used in conjunction with each other is invaluable in making program adjustments.

If teachers conduct ongoing educational assessment that takes place on a regular basis, then they can rearrange the aspects of instruction and shift the students' focus on progress. Moreover, specific assessments are more useful than global assessments because the first type provides students with an opportunity to see their own concrete improvement (Andersen et al. as cited in Johnson, 2010). Formative assessment also pertains to recent theories of learning and motivation as well as to perceiving the curriculum as a system consisting of numerous subsystems. Likewise, formative assessment has a significant impact on the kind of achievement goals internalized by learners.

These goals can be classified as performance objectives and mastery objectives. A performance-goal orientation is an essential component of the system dynamics curriculum because teachers underline the importance of comparison of students' abilities (Kennedy & Shiel, 2010). Educators actively engage with promoting and reinforcing performance goals by making student assessments public as well as offering rewards to students who outperform others. On the other hand, a mastery-goal orientation focuses on understanding, learning, and mastering new skills as well as undertaking challenges (Hassett & Curwood as cited in Johnson, 2010). The promotion of mastery goals occurs through the evaluation of student progress, as teachers are prone to treat mistakes as an integral part of the learning process.

While giving feedback for formative assessment, educators need to attribute results to students' persistent efforts and then investigate changes in instruction and learning tasks and assignments. In addition, teachers should consider the fact that formative assessment allows a relatively high level of student self-assessment (Airasian & Russell, 2008; Ford, 2008 as cited in Johnson, 2010). The latter is not solely a process of checking answers but is an engaging process in which learners monitor and assess the specificity of their thinking patterns. The main idea is to identify effective strategies that can improve understanding over time. In fact, self-assessment is a three-step process, as learners initially judge their own work, then identify gaps between current and desired performance, and implement further learning activities in order to improve their skills (Rupp & Lesaux, 2006; Vitullo & Jones, 2010 as cited in Johnson, 2010). Although teachers provide feedback, they can significantly encourage self-assessment by asking students relevant questions that help them to concentrate on the aspects of self-monitoring.

Students receive the most benefit from individual activities if teachers encourage them to correct their work before submission. Learners can also comprehend the importance of self-assessment as a method by considering certain dynamic models provided by teachers and by practicing peer assessment (Andersen et al. as cited in Johnson, 2010). Key elements of self-assessment are self-reflection and goal setting. With time and appropriate training, students can gradually assume a greater responsibility for assessing the extent to which they can reach learning targets. Teacher feedback can facilitate this process by providing numerous choices for students and asking proper questions.

In fact, many assessments take place throughout the instruction, within the classroom structure. For example, in many courses, summative evaluations are conducted to assess the students' learning. McMahon (1999) promotes a model of self-assessment throughout a course, whereby, it becomes the overall process of assessment. "The primary benefit of self-assessment becomes the promotion of critical thinking" (p. 553).

Another very popular assessment tool for educators is the pretest-posttest (McMullen & McMullen, 2009) analysis used at the beginning and end of a course to ascertain change in learning the content. Unfortunately, few studies (McMullen & McMullen, 2009; Tanner, 2005) have reported a significant change in students' critical thinking skills using this assessment procedure. However, per the authors' experience, it seems to be a good tool for assessing the student's retention of content information.

Rubrics are another popular assessment technique. Zane states that Analytic scoring rubrics have the potential to support constructivist learning theory more fully for at least 3 reasons:

1. Students can use rubrics to gain a better understanding of the targets of success. This may offer a framework for constructing their own knowledge and for understanding their skill levels;

2. Diagnostic rubrics can support metacognition by encouraging *self assessment* of their performance and may even *foster deeper self evaluation or reflection*; and

3. Analytic scoring can facilitate a supportive learning environment because the detailed criteria can foster more meaningful feedback from graders which can support subsequent remediation. (Zane, 2009, p. 91)

In general, a rubric is a rating system that is useful for determining the precise level of proficiency of students (Cutler III as cited in Johnson, 2010). Furthermore, if teachers allow students the opportunity to participate actively in the creation of assessment rubrics, they can further facilitate their learning experience. Rubrics are mainly used for language assignments that require an oral or written presentation from students. Educators need to design rubrics that adhere to the precise goals of instruction by considering the elements of systems thinking and system dynamics (Andersen et al. as cited in Johnson, 2010).

One of the common types of rubrics is that of holistic rubrics, which correspond to students' language performance. This ensures an entire impression of the teaching and learning process. The emphasis of holistic scoring is on the aspects students have mastered or their strengths on particular assignments. Additionally, educators must consider the importance of analytic rubrics that represent various components of performance. For instance, components for writing performance may include content, organization, grammar, and technical aspects (Kennedy & Shiel as cited in Johnson, 2010). Teachers need to score every component separately. The major benefit of employing analytic rubrics in the system dynamics curriculum is that educators can present different evaluations of different aspects. For instance, a given writing assignment might place greater importance on the component of content rather than on the component of mechanics. Another advantage of analytic rubrics is that they will give teachers relevant details about the strengths and weaknesses throughout the students' development of ideas in the classroom.

Primary trait rubrics present another important assessment technique, in which teachers focus on the presentation of a primary trait for optimal performance on classroom assignments. This assessment procedure is helpful for allowing educators to discuss the appropriateness of one element of the process of language performance. Likewise, it is a closely relevant way of scoring the writing and speaking performance of students (Mokhtari, Rosemary, & Edwards as cited in Johnson, 2010). Eventually, teachers can implement the assessment technique of multi-trait rubrics, whose essence is based on the assessment of more than one dimension. For instance, if teachers ask students to describe a picture, then a multi-trait rubric would be mostly concerned with the following dimensions: overall quality, fluency, and control of their presentation language.

Another popular assessment now being pursued is the portfolio that can either be in a hardcopy format or devised as e-portfolios. "The principal argument of the "improvement" movement is that it is only the assessment instruments assisting faculty in the classroom that are useful and that faculty are best served if they design and use their own assessments, such as portfolios (a recent favorite)" (Benjamin, 2012, p. 9). Portfolios are excellent learning tools that provide a way for students to value themselves as learners.

One of the problems of administering assessments is that the faculty either views them as an "add-on" or "after-the-fact" requirement to comply with directions from higher authority. "The faculty often sees the results as disconnected from classroom learning goals and practice. This makes it unlikely that the link between teaching and assessment will be established" (Chun, 2010, p. 23). Thus, the best way to assess the student's learning is through implementing formative assessments that play at particular points throughout the instruction. Below is an example of using varied assessment instruments to ensure learning has been accomplished throughout a course.

Scenario Example: The course is on devising a course using the ADDIE principles.

1. The students would be given a **pretest** that speaks to the ADDIE process, its components, and what each component is designed to discover.
2. The initial foundation content is then presented to the learner(s) on the ADDIE process.
3. Each section of the ADDIE process is done separately and graded separately to ensure that the learning outcomes have been achieved. With each section a **RUBRIC i**s devised for the grading.
4. The final product is combined and **presented orally**. The oral presentation and the final product will be graded **via a rubric. A post-test** will be administered and **compared to the pretest results.**
5. The final product will be included in a **portfolio on "Components required to Design Instruction"** that will include not only this product but various other research papers and related products completed under the Education Specialist curriculum.
6. The **student evaluation** will be completed at the end of the session.

SYNOPSIS

As stated in the introduction of this handbook, the content has just touched the surface of the information needed to design and deliver courses or curriculum in an ever-changing world which leans towards technology each day. In order to devise great instruction, one would have to make themselves knowledgeable in the types of interactive activities to employ within a course that makes it engaging, but yet not overwhelming. There is such as a thing as too many bells and whistles. So a good designer knows *how much* to incorporate, the *types of activities* that reinforces the content to be learned, and the strategies to use to assess *"did they learn what they were supposed to learn"*, and *how do I know that they know?* These are two very critical questions that must be answered when you devise instruction.

We hope the information we provided starts you easily on the path to designing instruction that is memorable for the learner. After all, that is really what is important, right?

REFERENCES

Aldrich, C. (2005). *Learning by doing: A comprehensive guide to simulations, computer games, and pedagogy in e-learning and other educational experiences.* San Francisco, CA: Pfeiffer.

Bagby, J., & Sulak, T. (2009). Strategies for promoting problem solving and transfer: A qualitative study. *Montessori Life, 21*(4), 38-42.

Bandura, A. (1977). *Social learning theory.* Englewood Cliffs, NJ: Prentice-Hall.

Baran, B. (2010). Experiences from the process of designing lessons with interactive whiteboard: ASSURE as a road map. *Contemporary Educational Technology, 1*(4), 367-380

Bartunek, J. M. (2007). Academic practitioner collaboration need not require joint or relevant research: Toward a relational scholarship of integration. *Academy of Management Journal, 50*(6), 1323-1333.

Bass, R. (1997). *A brief guide to interactive multimedia and the study of the United States.* Retrieved from http://www.georgetown.edu/crossroads/mltmedia.html

Bateman, T. S., & Snell, S. A. (2004). *Management: The new competitive landscape.* New York: McGraw-Hill Irwin.

Behaviorism. (n.d.). *Teaching guide for graduate student instructors.* Retrieved from http://gsi.berkeley.edu/resources/learning/behaviorism.html

Benjamin, R. (2008). The contribution of the collegiate learning assessment to teaching and learning. Retrieved from http://www.cae.org/content/pdf / The_Contribution_of_the_Collegiate_Learning _Assessment_to_Teaching_and_Learning_.pdf

Birzer, M. L., & Tannehill, R. (2001, June). A more effective training approach for contemporary policing. *Police Quarterly, 4*(2), 233-252.

Bloom B., Engelhart, M., Furst, E., Hill, W., & Krathwohl, D. (1956). *Taxonomy of educational objectives: The classification of educational goals.* Ann Arbor, MI: David McKay Inc..

Borthwick, A. F., Jones, D. R., & Wakai, S. (2003). Designing learning experiences within learner's zones of proximal development (ZPD): Enabling collaborative learning on-site and online. *Journal of Information Systems, 17*(1), 107-134.

Cheever, J. (2013). *What are learning styles?* Retrieved from http://www.life123.com/parenting/education/learning-styles/ what-are-learning-styles.shtml?o=2800&qsrc=999&ad=doub leDown&an=apn&ap=ask.com

Cherry, K. A. (2005). *Classical conditioning.* Retrieved from http://psychology.about.com/od/behavioralpsychology/a/ classcond.htm

Cherry, K. A. (2013). *Freud's Stages of psychosexual development.* Retrieved from http://psychology.about.com/od/ theoriesofpersonality/ss/pychosexualdev.htm

Clark, D. (2010). *Big dog and little dog juxtaposition.* Retrieved from http://www.nwlink.com/~donclark/agile/ agile_learning_design.html

Clark, R. (1999). *Building expertise: Cognitive methods for training and performance improvement.* Washington, DC: International Society for Performance Improvement.

Clark, R., & Mayer, R. E. (2011). *E-learning and the science of instruction* (3rd ed.).San Francisco, CA: Wiley & Sons.

Cô, J. E., & Levine, C. (1988). A critical examination of the ego identity status paradigm. *Developmental review, 8*(2), 147-184.

Cognitive Constructivism. (n.d.). *Teaching guide for graduate student instructors.* Retrieved from http://gsi.berkeley.edu/resources/learning/behaviorism.html

Considering the Curriculum. (n.d.). *Curriculum Development in Education* [Compact Disk]. MAE 505 Module 1: Touro University International Winter 2007.

Conway, J. (1997). *Educational technology's effect on models of instruction.* Retrieved from http://copland.udel.edu/~jconway/edst666.htm

Dijkstra, S. (2004). Curriculum, instruction, and media choice. In N. Seel & S. Dijkstra (Ed.), *Curriculum, plans, and processes in instructional design: International perspectives* (145-170). Mahwah, NJ: Erlbaum.

Dijkstra, S., Schott, F., Seel, N. M., & Tennyson, R. D. (1997). *Instructional design: International perspectives (Vol. 1).* Mahwah, NJ: Erlbaum.

Doll, R. C. (1996). *Curriculum improvement: Decision making and process.* Retrieved from http://www.multiage-education.com/russportfolio/curriculumtopics/curovierview.html

Driscoll, M. P. (2000). *Psychology of learning for instruction* (2nd ed.). Boston, MA: Pearson.

Duffy, T. M., & Kirkley, J. R. (Eds.). (2004). *Learner-centered theory and practice in distance education: Cases from higher education.* Mahwah, NJ: Erlbaum.

Duncan, S. L. (Spring 1996). Cognitive apprenticeship in classroom instruction: Implications for industrial and technical teacher education. *Journal of Industrial Teacher Education, 33*(25).

Eklund, J., & Woo, R. (1998). *A cognitive perspective for designing multimedia learning environments.* Paper presented at the ASCILITE '98 Conference Proceedings.

Facione, P. (1990). The Delphi Report. Executive Summary. *Critical thinking: A statement of expert consensus for purposes of educational assessment and instruction.* Millbrae, CA: Santa Clara University. (ERIC Doc. No. ED315423)

Farber, D. (n.d.) *Using simulations to facilitate learning.* Retrieved from http://coe.sdsu. edu/eet/articles/usflearning/index.htm

Feltovich, P. J., Spiro, R. J., Coulson, R. I., & Feltovic, J. (1996). Collaboration within and among minds: Mastering complexity, individually, and in groups. In T. Koschmann (Ed.), *CSCL: Theory and practice in an emerging paradigm.* Mahwah, NJ: Erlbaum.

Gagné, R. M. (1985). *The conditions of learning* (4th ed.). New York, NY: Holt, Rinehart & Winston.

Gokhale, A. A. (1995). Collaborative learning enhances critical thinking. *Journal of Technology Education, 7*(1), 1-2.

Gredler, M. E. (1997). *Learning and instruction: Theory into practice.* Upper Saddle River, NJ: Prentice-Hall, Inc.

Gutek. G. L. (2009). *New perspectives on philosophy and education.* Boston: Merrill.

Halnon, M. (2002). *2002 digital dictionary.* Retrieved from http://www.google.com/url?q=http://www.netaonline.org/pd-digitalglossary.rtf&sa=X&ei=hGwuTJ6dEdGQnwf0kc DfAw&ved=0CCcQpAMo&usg=AFQjCNFT5uj4E7MLe uEr4iCWLmITaGxU1w

Harrington, K. (2010). What Do You Want To Learn Today? *Learning & Leading with Technology, 37*(8), 48-48.

Hashim, Y. (1999). Are instructional design elements being used in module writing? *British Journal of Educational Technology, 30*(4), 341-361.

Instructional Design and Educational Media. (2006). A look into instructional design. Retrieved from http://www.wideopendoors.net

Iran-Nejad, A. (1995). Constructivism as substitute for memorization in learning: Meaning is created by learner. *Education, 116*(1), 16-34.

Johnson, S. (2011). *Digital tools for learning: 30 e-tools for collaborating, creating, and publishing across the curriculum.* Gainesville, FL: Maupin House

Johnson, S. E. (2010). *An action plan for achievement tests and performance test.* ED5014: School Organization. Prescott, AZ: North Central University.

Jonassen, D. H. (2006). *Modeling with technology. Mindtools for conceptual change.* (3rd ed.). Upper Saddle River, NJ: Pearson.

Jonassen, D. H., & Land, S. M. (Eds.). (2000). *Theoretical foundations of learning environments*. Mahwah, NJ: Erlbaum.

Kapoun, J. (2003). The use of PowerPoint in the library classroom: An experiment in learning outcomes. *Library philosophy and practice, 6*(1), 1-9.

Kidney, G. W., & Puckett, E. G. (2003). Rediscovering first principles through online learning. *Quarterly Review of Distance Education, 4*(3), 202-212.

Klein, S., Benjamin, R., Shavelson, R., & Bolus, R.(2007). *The collegiate learning* assessment: Facts and fantasies. Retrieved from http://www.collegiatelearniingassessment.org/files/CLA_Facts_and_Fantasies.pdf

Knowles, M. S. (1970). The modern practice of adult education: Andragogy versus pedagogy. New York, NY: Association Press.

Knowles, M. S. (1984). *Andragogy in action: Applying modern principles of adult learning* (1ˢᵗ ed.). San Francisco, CA: Jossey-Bass.

Knowles, M. S. (1990). *The adult learner: A neglected species* (4ᵗʰ ed.). Houston, TX: Gulf.

Knowles, M. S., Holton, E. F., & Swanson, R. A. (2011). *The adult learner: A definitive classic in adult education and human resource development* (7ᵗʰ ed.). Burlington, MA: Elsevier Inc..

Ku, K. Y. I. (2009). Assessing students' critical thinking performance: Urging for measurements using multi-response format. *Thinking Skills and Creativity, 4*, 70-76. doi:1.1016/j.tsc.2009.02.001

Kumar, M. (2006). Constructivist epistemology in action. *The Journal of Educational Thought, 40*(3), 247-262.

Kurt, S. (2010). Technology use in elementary education in Turkey: A case study. *New Horizons in Education,58*(1), 65-76.

Lattuca, L., & Stark, J. (2009). *Shaping the college curriculum: Academic plans in context.* San Francisco: Jossey-Bass.

Li, S., & Liu, D. (2005, Winter). The online top-down modeling model. *Quarterly Review of Distance Education, 6*(4), 343-359.

Linn, M. C., Slotta, J. D., & Baumgartner, E. (2000). *Teaching high school science in the information age: A review of courses and technology for inquiry-based learning.* Touro University International, Winter 2007, MAE514 Infusing Technology into the Classroom.

Lunce, L. M. (Spring/Summer, 2006). Simulations: Bringing the benefits of situated learning to the traditional classroom. *Journal of Applied Educational Technology, 3*(1), 37-41.

McAninch, A. C. (2006). Dewey's theory of reflective thinking: A needed reality check for teacher education. *The Journal of the Texas Association of Colleges for Teacher Education, 19*(4), 472-482.

McGriff, S. J. (2001). *Isd knowledge base / instructional design & development / instructional systems design models.* Retrieved from http://www.personal.psu.edu/faculty/ s/j/sjm256/portfolio/kbase/IDD/ISDModels.html

McNeil, S. (2006). *What is instructional design?* Retrieved from www.coe.uh.edu/courses/ cuin6373/whatisid.html

Merrill, M. D. (2002). First principles of instruction. *ETR&D, 50*(3), 43-59.

Mobile Learning. (n.d.). *Integrating mobile learning.* Retrieved from http://telr.osu.edu/mobilelearning/

Morrison, G. R., Ross, S. M., & Kemp, J. E. (2004). *Designing effective instruction* (4th ed.). Hoboken, NJ: Wiley.

Mueller, T. (2012). *Authentic assessment toolbox: Portfolios.* Retrieved from http://jfmueller.faculty.noctrl.edu/toolbox/portfolios.htm#whatis

Norton, R. E. (1997). *DACUM handbook* (2nd ed.). Columbus, OH: Center on Education and Training for Employment. The Ohio State University.

Norton, R. E. (2004). *The DACUM curriculum development process.* Columbus, OH: Center on Education and Training for Employment. The Ohio State University.

Petersen, S., & Cruz, L. (2004, May/Jun). What did we learn today? The importance of instructional alignment. *Strategies, 17*(5), 33-36.

Piaget, J. (1971). Science of education and the psychology of the child. New York, NY: Viking Press.

PriSim Business War Games. (2004). Retrieved from http://www.prisim.com/

Rajala, J. B. (2003). Wireless technology in education. *The Journal (Technological Horizons In Education), 31*(3), 28.

Ramanathan, M., Chau, R., & Straubinger, R. M. (1997). Integration of Internet-Based technologies as learning tools in a pharmaceutical calculations course. *American Journal of Pharmaceutical Education, 61*,141-148.

Reigeluth, C. M. (Ed.). (1999). Instructional-design theories and models: A new paradigm of instructional theory (Vol. II). Mahwah, NJ: Erlbaum.

Reiser, R. A. (2001). A history of instructional design and technology: Part II: A history of instructional design. *Educational Technology, Research and Development, 49*(2), 57-67.

Reyes, D. (1990). Models of instruction. *Clearing House, 63*(5), 214-220.

Roblyer, M. D. (2002). *Integrating instructional software into teaching and learning, Chapter 4.* Touro University International, Winter 2007, MAE514 Infusing Technology into the Classroom.

Rolls, A. (2007). *International perspectives on education* (Reference Shelf). New York: H. W. Wilson.

Shank, R. C., Berman, T. R., & Macpherson, K. A. (1999). Learning by doing. *Instruction-design theories and models: A new paradigm of instructional theory* (Vol. II, pp. 161-181). Mahwah, NJ: Erlbaum.

Schunk, D. H. (2004). Information processing (4th ed.). Learning theories, an educational perspective. New Jersey: Pearson.

Shelley, G. B., Cushman, T. J., Gunter, R. E., & Gunter, G. A. (2004). *Integrating technology in the classroom.* Boston: Shelly Cushman Series.

Sims, R., & Jones, D. (2002). Continuous improvement through shared understanding: Reconceptualising instructional design for online learning. In A. Williamson, C. Gunn,

A. Young, & T. Clear (Eds.), *Winds of change in the sea of learning*. Proceedings of the 19th Annual Conference of the Australasian Society for Computers in Learning in Tertiary Education. Auckland, NZ: UNITEC Institute of Technology. Retrieved from http://www.ascilite.org.au/ conferences /auckland02/proceedings/papers/162.pdf

Skinner, B. F. (1974). *About behaviorism.* New York, NY: Knopf.

Smith, L. W., & Van Doren, D. C. (2004). The reality-based learning method: A simple method for keeping teaching activities relevant and effective. *Journal of Marketing Education, 26*(1), 66-74. doi: 10.1177/0273475303262353

Smith, P. L., & Ragan, T. J. (1999). *Instructional design.* (2nd ed.). Hoboken, NJ: Wiley.

Social Constructivism. (n.d.). *Teaching guide for graduate student instructors.* Retrieved from http://gsi.berkeley.edu/resources/ learning/social.html

Spector, J. M., Ohrazda, C., Van Schaack, A., & Wiley, D. A. (Eds.) (2005). *Innovations in instructional technology: Essays in honor of M. David Merrill.* Mahwah, NJ: Erlbaum.

Spiro, R. J., Coulson, R. L., Feltovich, P. J., & Anderson, D. K. (1988). *Cognitive flexibility theory: Advanced knowledge acquisition in ill-structured domains* (Tech. Re. No. 441). Cambridge, MA: Bolt, Beranek, and Newman. Retrieved from ERIC database. (ED302821)

Spiro, R. J., Feltovich, P. J., Jacobson, M. J., & Coulson, R. I. (1995). Cognitive flexibility, constructivism, and hypertext: Random access instruction for advanced knowledge acquisition in ill-structured domains. In L.P. Steffe & J. Gale (Eds.) *Constructivism in instruction*. Hillsdale, NJ: Erlbaum.

Starko, A. J. (2005). Creativity in the classroom. Schools of curious delight (3rd ed.). Mahwah, NJ: Erlbaum.

Technology. (2010). In *Merriam-Webster Online Dictionary*. Retrieved from http://www.merriam- webster.com/ dictionary/technology.

Tennyson, R. D., & Spector, J. M. (1998). System dynamics technologies and future directions in instructional design [Electronic Version]. *Journal of Structural Learning & Intelligent Systems, 13*, 89.

Thornburg, D. (2002). *The new basics: Education and the future of work in the telematic age*. Alexandria, VA: ASCD.

Tonn, B., Hemrick, A., & Conrad, F. (2006, September). Cognitive representations of the future: Survey results. *Futures, 38*(7), 810-829.

Trapp, P. (2005, Mar/Apr). Engaging the body and mind with the spirit of learning to promote critical thinking. *Continuing Education in Nursing, 36*(2), 73-77.

Vander Zanden, J. W. (2003). *Human development* (7th ed.) (Rev. ed.). New York, NY: McGraw-Hill.

Visser, L., Visser, Y., & Schlosser, C. (2003, Winter). Critical thinking in distance education and traditional education. *Quarterly Review of Distance Education,4*(4), 401-408.

Vygotsky, L. S. (1978). *Mind in society*. Cambridge, MA: Harvard University.

Wallen, E., Plass, J. L., & Brunken, R. (2005). The function of annotations in the comprehension of scientific texts:

Cognitive load effects and the impact of verbal ability. *ETR&D, 53*(3), 59-72.

White, C. R., Carson, J. L., & Wilbourn, J. M. (1991). *Training and effectiveness of an M-16 Rifle Simulator. Military Psychology, 3.* Retrieved from http://web. ebscohost.com/ehost/detail?vid=6&hid=16&sid=292ed506 95a7-4b3c-9c26-e5291f1cc195%40SRCSM1

Whitney, K. (2004). *Performance-based simulations: Customizable tools.* Retrieved from http://www.clomedia.com/content/ templates/clo_specialreport.asp? articleid=670&zoneid=138

Wiig, E. H., & Wiig, K. M. (1999). Conceptual learning considerations. *Knowledge Research Institute, Inc.* Retrieved from Http://www.krii.com/downloads/ conceptual_learning.pdf

Wilson, L. O. (2005). *Wilson's curriculum pages – What is curriculum? and what are the types of curriculum?* Retrieved from http://www.uwsp.edu/education/lwilson/curric/ curtyp.htm

Winters, E. (2002). Cross cultural communication for business: Glossary. Retrieved from http://www.bena.com/ewinters/ Glossary.html

Wittrock, M. C. (1989, Fall). Generative processes of comprehension. *Educational Psychologist, 24*(4), 345-376.

Yates, R. (2000). Curriculum overview. Retrieved from http://www.multiage-education.com / russportfolio/ curriculumtopics/curovierview.html

Zisman, A. (1995). *Compton's interactive encyclopedia.* Retrieved from http://www.zisman. ca/Articles/1995/Comptons.html

APPENDIX A. DIGITAL TOOLS FOR EDUCATORS

Technology's Impact on Teaching and Learning

Technology is a major force that has touched almost every aspect of life with computers and continues to have a powerful effect on educational practices (Rolls, 2007). So, what is this thing called technology? Prior to initiating a discussion on technology's impact on teaching and learning, the author deems it is necessary to first define technology. Technology is defined as "the practical application of knowledge (especially in a particular area), a capability given by the practical application of knowledge, a manner of accomplishing a task especially using technical processes, methods, or knowledge, and the specialized aspects of a particular field of endeavor (Technology, 2010, para. 1). Bateman and Snell (2004) views technology as the methods, processes, systems, and skills used to transform resources into products. With the above definitions in mind, one could possibly conclude that technology involves knowledge-the know-how behind technological innovation; technology involves activities-what people do; and technology involves a process-begins with a need and ends with a solution.

Technology can be used to create highly motivating learning environments that help students acquire early habits of serious thought and work necessary for intellectual development (Rolls, 2007). According to the Office of Technology Assessment (as cited in Kurt, 2010), "effectively incorporate technology into the teaching and learning process is one of the most important steps the nation can take to make the most of past and continuing investments in educational technology" (p. 66). Technology in a learning environment is also designed to help bridge the gap between school and real intellectual work (Rolls, 2007). Thornburg (2002), contends that educators must identify the skills students will need to thrive in the workplace of today and tomorrow in order to explore how to modify the curriculum and measure student mastery.

School curricula often present the standard subjects in an intellectually impoverished and uncompelling way, teaching ways of thinking and doing that are distinctly different from those used by practitioners (Rolls, 2007). Education should be directed to grounding knowledge in experience and in contexts of use, and Technology can be used to create and support the knowledge sources, learning environments, and instructional tools necessary to foster this kind of cognitive development (Harrington, 2010). Technology tools can be made transparent and accessible to students for exploration, study, and analysis.

Instructional design incorporating technology tools can contribute greatly to motivating an understanding of the issues at the heart of learning and thinking within all disciplines

(Rolls, 2007). Educators looking to energize classroom instruction that enhances teaching and learning must include technology tools such as computers, laptops, wireless laptops, and tablet PCs. Additionally, Internet activities and Hypermedia can enhance teaching and learning in the classroom.

Internet-Based Activities Used to Foster Student Learning

According to Ramanathan, Chau, and Straubinger (1997), "There are many aspects of the Internet that may prove useful in education and a wide range of software tools are at the disposal of instructors" (p. 141). Three Internet activities used in the classroom to foster student learning are problem solving, collaborative learning, and conceptual learning.

Problem Solving.

Problem solving is the evaluation of relevant material to explore problems of everyday life (Rolls, 2007). Problem solving methods provide greater involvement for students, which develop growth in problem solving skills and provide a better understanding (Bagby & Sulak, 2009). This type of learning helps one to think critically, analyze problems, and to find and use appropriate leaning resources. According to Gutek (2009), "education was truly progressive when children learned to think reflectively by formulating plans, gathering evidence pertinent to the problem, and avoiding being diverted into incidental and irrelevant matters" (p. 87).

The Internet offers a number of resources to help students develop problem-solving skills. These skills are relevant to the student because they allow the student to explore problems that are applicable in the world outside of the schoolhouse. A problem solving technique is brainstorming, which members communicating on a web cam generate as many ideas and solutions about a problem as possible (Schunk, 2004).

Collaborative Learning.

According to Gokhale (1995), "The term "collaborative learning" refers to an instruction method in which students at various performance levels work together in small groups toward a common goal" (p. 1). The goals of collaborative learning are to learn the material, work together, and respect each member's contributions and intelligence (Conway, 1997). The Internet provides access to multimedia sources such as encyclopedias where the students can download images and sounds for use in presentations. Search engines like Ask.com and Google provide rapid access to information on any subject.

According to Conway (1997), there are three basic variations of the collaborative student team:

1. Student Teams Achievement Divisions – where students help team members to learn the required material. Teams are evaluated with improvement scores based on how much the individual students have improved on their past scores;

2. Jigsaw – students become experts in an area and then teach the other students that material; and

3. Group Investigation – students choose a subject for investigation and conduct a presentation of their findings.

The active exchange of ideas within these small groups not only increase interest among the participants but also promotes critical thinking. Gokhale (1995) purported, collaborative leaning can only be effective when educators view teaching as a process of developing and enhancing students' ability to learn. The instructor's role is to serve as a facilitator rather than transmit information, which involves creating and managing meaningful learning experiences and stimulating students' thinking through real world problems (Gokhale).

Conceptual Learning.

The Internet provides a wealth of tools for learning basic concepts of well structured subjects such as science, math, foreign languages, social sciences, and other subjects (Conway, 1997). However, these tools are less satisfactory for subjects such as composition and reading comprehension. There are two techniques available on the Internet for teaching conceptual learning. The first technique is drill and practice (Wiig & Wiig, 1999). This provides a student with an opportunity to practice basic skills with the computer acting as the controller to correct the student and provide rewards if they perform a task successfully. This allows the student to practice as long as they wish while the teacher helps others.

The second technique uses tutorial programs that allow a student to learn without any help from a teacher or other resources other than the program (Wiig & Wiig, 1999). Some of these tutorials work in a linear method that is the same for all users. A branching tutorial can assess when the student has mastered a concept and then may skip some sections and move on to different material. The Virtual Resource Site for Teaching with Technology lists Internet sites of conceptual subjects that provide teaching opportunities by using databases, maps, images, applets, animations, text, and repositories (Wiig & Wiig).

Hypermedia in the Classroom

According to Shelly, Cashman, Gunter, and Gunter (2004), individualized instruction and exploration is the essence of interactivity and is designed to enrich the educational experience. The author will expound on two hypermedia tools that enhance teaching and learning in the classroom: interactive hypermedia and authoring hypermedia technology.

Interactive Hypermedia.

Interactive hypermedia is a form of hypertext whereby text, graphics, images, animation, video, and audio are accessible by links that will take the user to specific references. The user controls or navigates the way they go through the material.

Halnon (2002) offers the following definition: Also known as, "interactive multimedia," this format allows random access to information in a program. Unlike normal video, which starts at an unchangeable beginning and proceeds through to a predetermined end, hypermedia, allows the viewer to control a program's pace, explore sections within it, and determine where the beginning and the end are. An interactive multimedia title lets students explore programs at their own pace (Halnon).

Bass (1997) offers several reasons why interactive hypermedia should be used in the classroom:

1. Access to large amounts of material in multiple forms in an integrated environment
2. Storage capacity of thousands of books and films
3. Individual control of sequence and speed
4. Hypermedia involves more of the senses and improves memory

An example of an interactive hypermedia system is the *Compton's Interactive Encyclopedia* (Zisman, 1995). This encyclopedia offers the user audio, images, sounds, maps and methods of manipulating those maps, hypertext links to other articles, and other features. This allows the user to explore subjects at their own pace and by their own method.

An example of multimedia use in the classroom setting would be in a science class where students are studying the human body. Shelly et al. (2004) described a program named Ultimate Human Body by DK Multimedia that allows students to interact and learn the human body. By clicking on the heart, they can hear the heart beat in action and learn all the important functions of the heart.

Authoring Hypermedia.

This type of system allows the user to create interactive hypermedia documents using sounds, images, graphics, text, animation, and videos. The user can create a hypermedia document for use by others or for a presentation. The writer can create places for users to input information or answer questions. The hypermedia document can be a simple presentation with pictures and sounds or a complex simulation of a process or procedure.

An example of authoring hypermedia used in the classroom would be a group of students given an assignment to create a hypermedia presentation to the other students on a Civil War battle. The students could use maps that depict the deployment of forces, pictures of battlefields or equipment, videos from movies or documentaries of the Civil war, or the sounds of battle. Each of these would help the presentation to come alive for the audience and be much more memorable.

Kapoun (2003) states problems of authoring hypermedia include the complexity of the software. Even simple programs take time to learn to a level of acceptable complexity. Another problem Kapoun discusses is that the author may use too much hypermedia such as sounds or graphics that interferes with the purpose of the presentation.

Classroom Learning with Simulations

Computer based instructional simulations are powerful instructional delivery tools that allows instructors to provide learners with authentic learning environments to practice, feedback about learner performances (Lunce, 2006). A well designed simulation and instruction provides an effective rich learning environment for students. Simulations are a means for achieving depth and variety in learning (Aldrich, 2005).

Roblyer (2002) discusses three simulations: physical, process, and situational that reflect engaged learning (Slide 10).

Physical.

A physical simulation is a device used for training purposes that represents the actual equipment that would be used in a real-world setting. The simulation must look, feel, and sound like the real thing for effective training to occur. The purpose of the physical simulation is to train the user to respond to real-world situations without incurring the cost, time, or danger inherent in training with the actual equipment (Roblyer, 2002).

The United States Army uses an effective classroom physical simulation that replicates firing an M16 rifle (White, Carson, & Wilbourn, 1991). This system uses a full size replica of an M16 that fires a laser at a monitor showing targets. Each time the simulator is fired a screen shows the user where the round hit. Using this information the user adjusts their point of aim until the target is hit. This simulator has a number of features that enable the user to train on a target range with pop-up targets, paper targets, or a combat scenario with enemy targets moving at various ranges. The simulator emits a sound when fired and has a recoil that forces the user to bring the weapon back on target. Marksmanship trainers can use the system to train students on steady-hold factors, point of aim, and other marksmanship issues. This system saves time and money by not having to go to the range or fire actual ammunition. The system is also safer. One disadvantage is that only one person at a time can use the system unless multiple systems are available.

Process.

Process simulation is marked by gradual changes through a series of states. This type of simulation is used in business, science, and engineering to model a process after a change has been introduced. The end state of the process is then evaluated to see if the change was beneficial or negative (Smith & Van Doren, 2004).

An example of this type of simulation in the classroom is the *Interactive Physics and Working Model* as described by Linn, Slotta, and Baumgartner (2000). This program allows students to conduct physics experiments without the costs or requirements necessary in an actual laboratory. Students create systems and then change the variables to see the results of the changes. These experiments can be performed a number of times during a classroom period because the experiments do not have to be set up in real-time. The results can be displayed graphically. This program also offers preconfigured simulations that can be used in physics classes to meet most curriculum requirements (Linn, et al.).

Process simulations are only as accurate as the data that is used to program the process. Most use sophisticated statistical calculations to derive the results. If the data is accurate to one decimal place then the result is accurate to one decimal place. This means that the results of a simulation may not always produce the desired results when done in real-world environments.

Situational.

Lunce (2006) stated, "situational simulations generally model human behavior focusing on attitudes of individuals or groups in specific settings. These simulations often employ role playing as a vehicle to allow students to explore different options and decision paths" (p. 38). Situational simulations place the user in an environment where their actions directly affect the situation. The goal of most situational simulations is to learn how to effectively deal with resources, human, or capital. An example of a situational simulation is the PriSim Business War Games (PriSim, 2004). This business simulation models the, "...complete operations of a working and growing business" (Whitney, 2004, para. 5). This simulation is customized for an individual company and requires that company's members to make all decisions that would normally have to be made in the business world for a new product or service. Teams compete against each other to produce the best results. The advantage of the simulation is that errors in forecasting, resource procurement, sales management, and many other areas are demonstrated in the simulation and can be corrected without losing time or money (Whitney, 2004, para. 5). Situational simulations are usually designed to be run several times with each participant in the simulation scenario playing a different role in each iteration. Situational simulations, because of their open-ended design and complexity of modeling human behavior, tend to be the most difficult type of simulation to design and utilize effectively (Lunce, 2006).

Engaged Learning

Farber (n.d.) stated simulations, "...enhances problem solving and decision making skills" (Summary). The article discusses transfer of knowledge using computer-based simulations as quicker and effective as traditional methods (Farber, n.d., Studies on Transfer of Learning). This is because students perform tasks and experiment with variables, and see the results rather than just discussing the subjects. Educators must be prudent with designing, to maximize the use of technology as they set objectives and design lessons for the classroom.

Wireless Technology in the Classroom

Wireless technology has unlimited potential in the classroom. Wireless access in learning offers new opportunities for engaging learners. According to Rajala (2003), "It would be counterproductive for the 21st century student to be harnessed to a computer lab--handcuffed to place and time for learning to occur" (p. 1).

Mobile Laptop Computers.

Wireless laptops can help to eliminate many of the barriers, obstacles and inconveniences that have contributed to teacher reluctance in the past, but the focus of use must be on curriculum and learning (Mobile Learning, n.d.). Rajala (2003) and Mobile Learning (n.d.) agree on the following advantages of wireless technology in the classroom:

- Portability. Laptops are fairly lightweight--they can easily and conveniently be wheeled from room to room on a cart or be moved to wherever student learning is taking place--while PDAs fit inside your pocket.
- Anytime, anywhere use. Providing you remain within the range of your designated wireless base, students can use wireless laptops or PDAs to access the Internet from just about anywhere. However, you would preferably want any electronic equipment to steer clear of areas with dirt, dust, food, etc.
- Time savings. Think about how much time is in a class period, then consider the time lost by having students go to and from the computer lab. You gain valuable learning time when the technology comes to the students.
- High comfort level. The familiar surroundings combined with the small size of a laptop or PDA add up to both students and teachers being comfortable and relaxed - and perhaps not feeling overwhelmed by big desktop computers that neither student nor teacher can see around.

Using wireless technology provides greater learning opportunities because of the increased access to information. Wireless technology fills a need that a traditional computer lab or limited numbers of desktop computers in classrooms cannot satisfy. Students benefit from using the mobile lab computers, because it gives them the opportunity to combine the resources they have in their classroom with the technology resources they need to complete assignments (Rajala, 2003). The more comfortable and familiar we make the classroom experience with new technologies, the more likely we are to win enthusiastic use.

Creating and Engaging Your Course with Technology

Creating an engaging course with e-tools and activities allows your course to become relevant to your learners. In the learning environments of today, you may be teaching a mixture of Generation X (1965-1981), Net Generation (1977-1997), and the Millenniums (1980-2000). Each of these categories of learners has a different level of understanding and use of technological tools. Thus, when you devise your instruction using e-tools it will take some innovative teaching strategies to "norm" the levels of learning so you do not lose any students in the process of the course. Johnson (2011) suggested there were 5 ways to assess the use of digital products.

1. Because the courses that will be developed utilizing the e-tools or software products that will enhance learning, the instructor should "identify, incorporate, and engage their audiences" (p. 27).
2. Instructors must fully understand the content in order to connect it to the learner's world. In other words, relevance is critical!
3. Instructors must reflect on the creation process of the course and its components from the very beginning of the course all the way through to its inception. Reflection at each stage allows the designer to revise,

modify and connect to the learner in the activities that they choose to incorporate and in the e-tools that enhance the learning of each concept.

4. "Keep the focus on the content and the process, not the tool" (p. 30). The e-tool or software that you use never takes the place of the instructor, only assists the instructor to enhance learning the content in an efficient and more effective way.

Justify your choice. Always pick the best e-tool or software that compliments teaching the content. Always ask yourself, "Is this the best e-tool or software that will best illustrate the concept that I am trying to teach, and why?" There are so many tools via the Internet that can be downloaded for free and used to complement your instruction. However, this can be overwhelming. **Web 2.0 Guru website** is a list of numerous types of software and websites that assist the instructor to make engaging presentations to accompany your content. The resources listed below are some of the most popular for use by instructors and students when accomplishing assignments.

Mindtools: "Mind tools do not necessarily reduce information processing (i.e., make the task easier), rather, their goal is to make effective use of the mental efforts of the learners" (Jonassen, 2006, p. 21).

1. Inspiration (30 day free trial): This software is one of the leaders in devising various packages that will assist learners and instructors to create mind maps, concept maps, graphic organizers, process flow charts and other

diagrams. It encourages creativity and taps into the power of visual thinking as well as critical thinking. Inspiration9 is the latest version for adult learning for mind mapping. InspireData (also created by Inspiration) is a data analysis tool which allows the student to create charts, graphs, to improve the learner's analytical skills.

2. Webspiration (30 day free trial): Webspiration is much like Inspiration as far as a mind-mapping tool. However, it is designed for colleges and professionals, and allows online collaboration with teams or colleagues. One can create mind maps, concepts maps, and other visual thinking models, as well as devise outlines and reports to share or collaborate with others online.

3. Prezi (free online): This is starting to become the preferred designing tool for creating engaging presentations. Unlike Power Point, Prezi uses a single canvas rather than individual slides to create non-linear presentations that can zoom in and out of a visual map. To the left of the screen, a path is created whereby different objects and frames can be defined and moved into the order that is desired in the presentation.

4. Graphsy (free online)/Visio (free 60 day trial/Creatly (free online): These are all programs that allow you to create graphs or diagrams and share them collaboratively via web sharing.

5. Cacoo (free online) and Bubbles.us (free online): These are also free drawing tools whereby you can create maps, diagrams, and charts via brainstorming techniques.

Assessment tools:

6. Rubrics (free online): Rubrics are designed and based on designing instruction that is task oriented. Performance-based tasks require performance-based assessments in which the actual student performance is assessed through a product, such as a completed project or work that demonstrates levels of task achievement. A rubric allows one to align the grading to the outcomes in a matrix from good to bad.

7. Portfolios: "Some suggest that portfolios are not really assessments at all because they are just collections of previously completed assessments. But, if we consider *assessing* as gathering of information about someone or something for a purpose, then a portfolio is a type of assessment. Sometimes the portfolio is also evaluated or graded, but that is not necessary to be considered an assessment" (Mueller, 2012, (p. 1).

8. Student Evaluations: These are used frequently in colleges/universities but should be created with care. Most student evaluations really only evaluate the instructor, not the content learned. Thus, when you create a student evaluation you should be cognizant of the learning outcomes and create the questions to address the extent of learning that can be shown versus whether or not they liked the course.

9. Journals and writing exemplars: These certainly can be used as assessments but there has to be a criteria assigned

to them. Here is where the rubric can be devised and used in concert with these to maximize the assessment data that will be obtained from these assessment instruments.

Animations: There are numerous software applications that can be used to animate your projects; however, we will only address one that seems to be extremely popular. Camtasia (to include Camtasia Studio & Snagit): With this software you can create professional videos from your screen and from PowerPoint presentations. Camtasia provides a large amount of transitions and animation effects.

The above products are just a few that can be used by an educator to *bring life* into the classroom and into the projects. These allow you to engage the learner in various ways and tap into their preferred learning styles.

APPENDIX B: ABCD MODEL

The ABCD model for writing objectives

Introduction

- Objectives will include 4 distinct components: Audience, Behavior, Condition and Degree.
- Objectives must be both observable and measurable to be effective.
- Use of words like *understand* and *learn* in writing objectives are generally not acceptable as they are difficult to measure.
- Written objectives are a vital part of instructional design because they provide the roadmap for designing and delivering curriculum.
- Throughout the design and development of curriculum, a comparison of the content to be delivered should be made to the objectives identified for the program. This process, called *performance agreement*, ensures that the final product meets the overall goal of instruction identified in the first level objectives.

Characteristics of objectives

- Observable and measurable
- Unambiguous
- Results oriented / clearly written / specific
- Measurable by both quantitative and qualitative criteria
- Communicate a successful learning in behavioral terms
- Written in terms of performance
- May be presented in 2 levels: 1st level and 2nd level
  - 1st level: identify the overall goal of the instruction for the program or instructional event
    - Sometimes called terminal objectives
  - 2nd level: identify the goals required to meet the 1st level objectives
    - Sometimes called enabling objectives

Samples

- Given a standard sentence, the English 101 student should be able to identify the noun and verb without error.
- Given an assortment of EMS equipment to pick from, the paramedic should be able to identify all of the equipment necessary to perform rapid sequence intubation without error.
- The EMT-B participant in this pediatric workshop should be able to identify at least 4 warning signs of

possible child abuse from a family member's interview that contains 5 warning signs.

4 Parts of an ABCD Objective

- Audience
- Behavior
- Condition
- Degree
    - The objective does not have to be written in this order (ABCD), but it should contain all of these elements

Audience

- Describe the intended learner or end user of the instruction
- Often the audience is identified only in the 1st level of objective because of redundancy
- Example: The paramedic refresher participant...
- Example: The EMT-B student...
- Example: The prehospital care provider attending this seminar...

Behavior

- Describes learner capability
- Must be observable and measurable (you will define the measurement elsewhere in the goal)
- If it is a skill, it should be a real world skill

- The "behavior" can include demonstration of knowledge or skills in any of the domains of learning: cognitive, psychomotor, affective, or interpersonal
- Example: … should be able to write a report…
- Example: …should be able to describe the steps…
  - Cognitive domain
    - Emphasizes remembering or reproducing something which has presumably been learned
    - Deal with what a learner should know, understand, comprehend, solve, spell, critique, etc.
  - Psychomotor domain
    - Emphasizes some muscular motor skill, some manipulation of material and objects, or some act that requires a neuromuscular coordination
    - Concerned with how a learner moves or controls his/her body
  - Affective domain
    - Composed of two different types of behaviors: reflexive (attitudes) and voluntary reactions and actions (values)
    - Stages: perception, decision, action and evaluation
  - Interpersonal domain
    - Emphasizes learner skills (not attitude or knowledge) associated with interpersonal exchanges
    - How a learner interacts with others in a variety of situations

Condition

- Equipment or tools that may (or may not) be utilized in completion of the behavior
- Environmental conditions may also be included
- Example: ...given an oxygen wrench, regulator and D tank with oxygen...
- Example: ...given the complete works of William Shakespeare...
- Example: ...given the following environment: 10PM, snowing, temperature 0 degrees C...

Degree

- States the standard for acceptable performance (time, accuracy, proportion, quality, etc)
- Example: ... without error.
- Example: ... 9 out of 10 times.
- Example: ...within 60 seconds.

Review of ABCD Objectives

- Who is to exhibit the performance?
- What observable performance is the learner to exhibit?
- What conditions are provided for the learner at the time of evaluation?
- What constitutes a minimum acceptable response?

Performance Agreement

- Reiterative process where content is compared to objectives to determine if the content being delivered actually enables the student to meet the objectives
  - Be "reiterative" we mean that throughout the development of the course you should be reviewing to see if performance agreement is present. It is much easier to make minor adjustments as you go along than it is to make major changes in the end.
- If you cannot clearly see that the content being delivered meets the objectives then you must decide the following:
  - Rewrite the objectives to meet the content
  - Modify, enhance or remove the content to meet the objective as stated